The Giant Book of Unbelievable Facts

by
Jake Jacobs

* * * * *

Published by Jake Jacobs

1.

Nike was founded on January 25, 1964, as Blue Ribbon Sports by Bill Bowerman and Phil Knight.

2.

The company initially operated as a distributor for the Japanese shoe brand Onitsuka Tiger, now known as ASICS.

3.

The name "Nike" was adopted in 1971, inspired by the Greek goddess of victory.

4.

Nike's iconic "Swoosh" logo was designed by Carolyn Davidson in 1971 and purchased by Nike for $35.

5.

The first Nike shoe, the "Nike Cortez," was introduced in 1972 and quickly gained popularity among runners.

6.

In 1978, Nike introduced the revolutionary Air cushioning technology, which used air-filled pockets in the shoe's sole for enhanced comfort and performance.

7.

Nike became a publicly traded company in 1980, with its initial public offering (IPO) on the New York Stock Exchange.

8.

The famous "Just Do It" slogan was coined in 1988 and has become synonymous with Nike's brand identity.

9.

In 1989, Nike launched the Air Jordan line of basketball shoes in partnership with basketball legend Michael Jordan, revolutionizing the sneaker industry.

10.

Nike expanded its product offerings beyond footwear and started manufacturing athletic apparel in the late 1970s.

11.

The Nike brand became globally recognized in the 1990s, driven by innovative marketing campaigns and endorsement deals with high-profile athletes.

12.

Nike signed a groundbreaking endorsement deal with basketball player Michael Jordan in 1984, launching the highly successful Air Jordan brand.

13.

Nike's sponsorship of the 1996 Olympic Games in Atlanta, Georgia, solidified its status as a leading global sportswear brand.

14.

Nike faced controversies and criticism over the years, including labor and human rights issues in its overseas factories.

15.

The company has taken steps to improve its labor practices and environmental sustainability through initiatives like the Nike Grind program, which recycles old shoes into new products.

16.

Nike has collaborated with numerous influential designers, celebrities, and brands to create limited-edition and highly sought-after sneaker collections.

17.

Nike's annual revenue surpassed $1 billion for the first time in 1986, and it has continued to grow significantly since then.

18.

Nike has a long history of supporting and sponsoring various sports teams, athletes, and sporting events worldwide.

19.

Nike became the official apparel and footwear supplier for the National Football League (NFL) in 2012, replacing Reebok.

20.

The company has a strong presence in the basketball market, with endorsement deals with top NBA players and sponsorship of basketball leagues worldwide.

21.

Nike introduced its groundbreaking Flyknit technology in 2012, which uses a single thread to create a lightweight, form-fitting shoe upper.

22.

Nike launched the "Nike+ ecosystem" in 2006, combining wearable technology and mobile apps to track and analyze athletic performance.

23.

Nike's iconic Air Max line, first introduced in 1987, features visible air cushioning units in the shoe's sole.

24.

Nike has a significant impact on popular culture, with its products often featured in movies, music videos, and fashion trends.

25.

Nike's headquarters, known as the "Nike World Campus," is located in Beaverton, Oregon, and spans over 400 acres.

26.

Nike has a strong focus on social and environmental sustainability, setting goals to reduce its carbon footprint and improve supply chain practices.

27.

Nike has acquired several other companies and brands over the years, including Converse, Hurley, and Umbro.

28.

Nike has a dedicated research and development team, known as Nike Innovation, focused on creating new technologies and materials for its products.

29.

The Nike Mag, a shoe inspired by the self-lacing shoes worn by Marty McFly in the movie "Back to the Future II," was released as a limited edition in 2011.

30.

Nike has sponsored multiple marathons and running events globally, including the iconic Nike Women's Marathon in San Francisco.

31.

Nike has a strong presence in the soccer market, sponsoring top clubs, national teams, and players worldwide.

32.

Nike launched the Nike FuelBand in 2012, a wearable fitness tracker that measures daily activity levels and encourages users to reach their fitness goals.

33.

Nike's advertising campaigns have won numerous awards and are known for their creativity and impactful messages.

34.

Nike has faced controversies related to athlete endorsements, including high-profile scandals involving athletes like Lance Armstrong and Oscar Pistorius.

35.

Nike has a dedicated team of designers and developers who work closely with athletes to create performance-enhancing products.

36.

Nike has a robust online presence, with its e-commerce platform offering a wide range of products and personalized shopping experiences.

37.

Nike has been at the forefront of innovation in footwear, introducing features like lightweight materials, cushioning systems, and adaptive fit technologies.

38.

Nike sponsors various youth sports programs and initiatives to promote active lifestyles and participation in sports.

39.

Nike's famous "Just Do It" campaign was launched in 1988 and has become one of the most recognized advertising slogans globally.

40.

Nike has a strong commitment to diversity and inclusion, with initiatives promoting gender equality, LGBTQ+ rights, and racial justice.

41.

Nike has collaborated with artists, musicians, and designers to create limited-edition sneaker collections that blend fashion and sportswear.

42.

Nike has a strong presence in the skateboarding industry, sponsoring professional skateboarders and producing skateboarding-specific footwear and apparel.

43.

Nike introduced the Nike FlyEase technology in 2015, designed to make shoes more accessible for people with disabilities.

44.

Nike has a history of sponsoring major sporting events, including the FIFA World Cup, the Olympic Games, and the NBA All-Star Game.

45.

Nike has a significant presence in the golf industry, sponsoring professional golfers and manufacturing golf apparel and equipment.

46.

Nike has a robust corporate social responsibility program, supporting initiatives related to education, community development, and sustainability.

47.

Nike's famous slogan "There is no finish line" reflects its commitment to continuous innovation and improvement in the athletic footwear and apparel industry.

48.

Nike has a strong focus on athlete performance and has developed specialized footwear for various sports and activities.

49.

Nike operates numerous flagship stores worldwide, showcasing its latest products and providing immersive brand experiences for customers.

50.

Nike's iconic "swoosh" logo is one of the most recognizable and widely known logos in the world, representing the company's commitment to excellence and athletic achievement.

51.

Target was founded in 1902 as the Dayton Dry Goods Company by George D. Dayton in Minneapolis, Minnesota.

52.

The first Target store opened on May 1, 1962, in Roseville, Minnesota.

53.

The store's original name was "Target" because it aimed to provide a unique shopping experience by offering trendy, stylish, and affordable products.

54.

Target's iconic red bullseye logo was created in 1962 and has remained a recognizable symbol of the brand.

55.

The company officially changed its name to "Target Corporation" in 2000 to reflect its focus on becoming a national retail chain.

56.

Target introduced its own private label brands in the 1980s, including Archer Farms, Market Pantry, and Up & Up, offering customers a wide range of affordable options.

57.

In 1995, Target launched its website, becoming one of the first major retailers to embrace e-commerce.

58.

Target expanded beyond the United States for the first time in 2011, opening stores in Canada. However, the Canadian venture was ultimately unsuccessful, and Target closed its Canadian stores in 2015.

59.

Target's commitment to design and fashion is evident through its collaborations with renowned designers and brands, such as Isaac Mizrahi, Missoni, Lilly Pulitzer, and Hunter.

60.

The company is known for its stylish and well-designed stores, often featuring unique architectural elements and a clean, modern aesthetic.

61.

Target introduced its loyalty program, Target Circle, in 2019, offering customers exclusive deals, personalized recommendations, and other benefits.

62.

In recent years, Target has been focused on expanding its grocery offerings, with many stores featuring a full grocery section.

63.

Target's commitment to sustainability is evident through various initiatives, including energy-efficient store designs, waste reduction efforts, and eco-friendly product options.

64.

The company has a strong philanthropic presence, donating millions of dollars to support education, health, and social causes through the Target Foundation.

65.

Target has a long history of giving back to local communities through volunteer programs and partnerships with nonprofit organizations.

66.

Target was one of the first major retailers to implement a same-day delivery service, offering customers the convenience of getting their purchases quickly.

67.

Target's annual "Black Friday" sales events have become highly anticipated, with customers lining up outside stores to take advantage of the deals.

68.

Target expanded its product offerings to include electronics, home goods, furniture, beauty products, and more, becoming a one-stop shop for many customers.

69.

Target introduced its "Target Run" campaign in 2015, emphasizing the convenience and fun of shopping at Target for everyday essentials.

70.

The company has embraced digital technologies, offering features like in-app shopping, curbside pickup, and contactless payment options.

71.

Target has a strong commitment to inclusivity and diversity, with initiatives to promote a welcoming environment for employees and customers of all backgrounds.

72.

Target's collaborations with popular influencers and social media personalities have helped drive customer engagement and brand awareness.

73.

The company has been recognized for its efforts in responsible sourcing and ethical supply chain practices.

74.

Target operates an extensive online marketplace, allowing third-party sellers to reach customers through the Target website.

75.

Target has been recognized as one of the best places to work, with a focus on employee satisfaction, benefits, and career development.

76.

The company operates various store formats, including small-format stores in urban areas and larger superstores in suburban locations.

77.

Target's focus on affordability is reflected in its "Expect More, Pay Less" slogan, emphasizing its commitment to providing value to customers.

78.

Target has a strong presence in the home goods category, offering a wide range of stylish and affordable options for home decor and furnishings.

79.

The company has invested in technology and data analytics to improve the customer experience, offering personalized recommendations and promotions.

80.

Target has been at the forefront of using social media and digital marketing strategies to connect with customers and build brand loyalty.

81.

The company has embraced sustainable packaging practices, aiming to reduce waste and promote recycling.

82.

Target has received recognition for its efforts in diversity and inclusion, including being named one of the "Best Places to Work for LGBTQ Equality" by the Human Rights Campaign.

83.

The company has implemented various initiatives to reduce its carbon footprint, including energy-efficient lighting, solar power installations, and recycling programs.

84.

Target's commitment to social responsibility is demonstrated through its involvement in community development projects and disaster relief efforts.

85.

The company has expanded its international presence through partnerships with international retailers, allowing customers in select countries to access Target products online.

86.

Target operates a robust customer loyalty program, offering exclusive discounts, early access to sales, and personalized recommendations based on shopping history.

87.

Target has a strong focus on customer convenience, with services like online ordering, in-store pickup, and same-day delivery options.

88.

The company has been recognized for its efforts in promoting gender equality and women's empowerment, including partnerships with women-owned businesses and initiatives supporting female entrepreneurs.

89.

Target operates a successful wedding registry service, allowing couples to create personalized gift lists for their special day.

90.

The company has a dedicated team of designers who create exclusive and stylish products, ranging from clothing and accessories to home decor and furniture.

91.

Target has been a pioneer in integrating technology into the in-store experience, with features like self-checkout kiosks, digital price tags, and interactive displays.

92.

The company has implemented sustainable practices in its supply chain, such as reducing packaging waste and promoting responsible sourcing of materials.

93.

Target has a strong commitment to education, supporting initiatives that promote literacy and provide resources for teachers and schools.

94.

The company has received recognition for its commitment to corporate transparency and ethical business practices.

95.

Target's annual sales events, such as "Target Deal Days" and "Target Deal Week," offer customers significant discounts on a wide range of products.

96.

The company operates a robust online presence, with a user-friendly website and mobile app that offers seamless shopping experiences.

97.

Target has been recognized as a leader in customer service, with dedicated teams to assist customers and resolve any issues they may have.

98.

The company has implemented sustainable packaging practices, such as using recycled materials and reducing the use of single-use plastics.

99.

Target has embraced augmented reality (AR) technology, allowing customers to virtually try on makeup, furniture, and other products before making a purchase.

100.

The company's commitment to community engagement is reflected in its support for local businesses, nonprofit organizations, and community events.

101.

The C.A. Thayer is a historic schooner built in 1895, originally used for the lumber trade on the West Coast of the United States.

102.

The name "C.A. Thayer" comes from Clarence A. Thayer, a prominent lumberman who owned the vessel.

103.

The schooner was designed and built by Hans Ditlev Bendixsen, a renowned shipbuilder from Eureka, California.

104.

The C.A. Thayer is one of the last surviving examples of a West Coast lumber schooner, once a common sight along the Pacific coast.

105.

The schooner measures 219 feet in length and has a displacement of 453 gross tons.

106.

Initially, the C.A. Thayer was rigged as a three-masted schooner, but it was later converted to a two-masted fore-and-aft schooner rig.

107.

The vessel's hull is made of Douglas fir planks, which were fastened with iron spikes during its construction.

108.

The C.A. Thayer was primarily used to transport lumber from the Pacific Northwest to San Francisco and other West Coast ports.

109.

In 1912, the schooner was involved in a collision with another vessel, resulting in significant damage to its bow. It was repaired and continued its lumber trade.

110.

During its active years, the C.A. Thayer had a crew of about 15 to 18 men who handled the vessel's operations.

111.

The schooner's cargo capacity was approximately 500,000 board feet of lumber.

112.

The C.A. Thayer sailed through treacherous waters, including the notorious Cape Horn, known for its fierce storms and dangerous conditions.

113.

In the early 20th century, the C.A. Thayer was fitted with an auxiliary engine to aid in maneuvering and provide power when winds were unfavorable.

114.

The vessel played a significant role in the development of the West Coast lumber industry, transporting timber from remote areas to urban centers.

115.

In the 1920s, as the demand for lumber declined, the C.A. Thayer was converted into a floating codfish processing ship in Alaska.

116.

During its time as a fish-processing vessel, the schooner operated in Bristol Bay, processing the abundant codfish caught in the region.

117.

The C.A. Thayer was eventually retired from service in 1950 and fell into disrepair.

118.

In the 1980s, the vessel was acquired by the San Francisco Maritime National Historical Park and underwent an extensive restoration.

119.

The restoration of the C.A. Thayer involved replacing rotted wood, reinforcing the hull, and recreating the vessel's original appearance.

120.

The schooner's restoration was completed in 2009, and it is now part of the San Francisco Maritime National Historical Park's fleet of historic vessels.

121.

Today, the C.A. Thayer serves as a floating museum, offering visitors a glimpse into the rich maritime history of the West Coast.

122.

The schooner is open for public tours, allowing visitors to explore its deck, cabins, and cargo holds.

123.

The C.A. Thayer has been designated a National Historic Landmark and is listed on the National Register of Historic Places.

124.

The vessel is known for its distinctive red-hulled appearance and traditional sailing ship features, such as tall masts and a bowsprit.

125.

The C.A. Thayer has appeared in several films and television shows, including the Disney film "Pete's Dragon" (1977) and the TV series "Deadliest Catch."

126.

The schooner has participated in numerous maritime festivals and events, showcasing its historical significance and sailing capabilities.

127.

The C.A. Thayer is often used for educational programs, providing hands-on learning experiences for students and maritime enthusiasts.

128.

The vessel's restoration involved the use of traditional shipbuilding techniques and materials to preserve its historical authenticity.

129.

The C.A. Thayer is an iconic symbol of the West Coast maritime heritage and represents the heyday of the lumber industry.

130.

The schooner's sails, when fully rigged, span an impressive area, making it a majestic sight on the water.

131.

The C.A. Thayer is one of the few surviving examples of the once-thriving fleet of lumber schooners that played a vital role in the region's economic development.

132.

The vessel's restoration required meticulous research and collaboration with maritime historians and shipbuilders.

133.

The C.A. Thayer has been featured in maritime art and photography, capturing its elegance and historical significance.

134.

The schooner's deck offers panoramic views of the surrounding waters and landscapes, providing a unique vantage point for visitors.

135.

The C.A. Thayer represents the craftsmanship and skills of the shipbuilders and sailors who constructed and operated these iconic vessels.

136.

The schooner's preservation is a testament to the dedication of individuals and organizations committed to safeguarding maritime history.

137.

The C.A. Thayer's journey from a working lumber schooner to a museum ship highlights the evolving roles and functions of historic vessels.

138.

The vessel's interior showcases the living quarters and amenities provided to the crew during its active years.

139.

The C.A. Thayer's restoration process involved sourcing specialized materials, such as old-growth Douglas fir, to ensure historical accuracy.

140.

The schooner's presence in the San Francisco Maritime National Historical Park contributes to the vibrant maritime heritage of the area.

141.

The C.A. Thayer's story is intertwined with the natural resources of the Pacific Northwest, reflecting the region's historical reliance on timber.

142.

The vessel's size and design demonstrate the engineering ingenuity required to navigate the unpredictable waters of the Pacific Ocean.

143.

The C.A. Thayer's restoration relied on the expertise of skilled shipwrights, preserving traditional shipbuilding techniques for future generations.

144.

The schooner's sails, when unfurled, create a beautiful spectacle as they catch the wind and propel the vessel through the water.

145.

The C.A. Thayer's history offers insights into the challenges faced by sailors, from navigating treacherous coastlines to enduring harsh weather conditions.

146.

The vessel serves as a reminder of the human connection to the sea and the reliance on maritime transportation for trade and commerce.

147.

The C.A. Thayer's restoration project employed a diverse range of artisans and craftsmen, including woodworkers, metalworkers, and rigging specialists.

148.

The schooner's restored appearance showcases the attention to detail and craftsmanship of the original shipbuilders.

149.

The C.A. Thayer's presence in the San Francisco Bay Area attracts maritime enthusiasts and tourists from around the world.

150.

The schooner's ongoing preservation and interpretation contribute to a deeper understanding and appreciation of the maritime heritage of the West Coast.

151.

The California Powder Works Bridge is a historic truss bridge located in Santa Cruz, California.

152.

The bridge was originally constructed in 1872 to provide access to the California Powder Works facility, which was one of the largest gunpowder manufacturing plants in the United States at the time.

153.

The California Powder Works Bridge is one of the oldest surviving iron truss bridges in California.

154.

The bridge was designed by William H. Hall, a civil engineer who specialized in bridge construction during the late 19th century.

155.

The bridge spans the San Lorenzo River, connecting the California Powder Works facility to the surrounding area.

156.

The California Powder Works Bridge played a vital role in transporting materials, equipment, and personnel to and from the gunpowder manufacturing plant.

157.

The bridge's truss design provided structural strength and stability, allowing it to withstand heavy loads and river currents.

158.

The California Powder Works Bridge is approximately 200 feet long, with a single span crossing the river.

159.

The bridge's truss configuration consists of Pratt trusses, which are characterized by diagonal members in tension and vertical members in compression.

160.

The California Powder Works Bridge features decorative ironwork, including ornate railings and lattice patterns, adding to its visual appeal.

161.

The bridge's construction utilized wrought iron, a durable material that was commonly used in bridge building during the 19th century.

162.

The California Powder Works Bridge is an important reminder of the industrial history of Santa Cruz and its role in the production of gunpowder during the 19th century.

163.

The California Powder Works facility was established in 1861 to supply gunpowder for mining, construction, and agricultural purposes.

164.

The gunpowder produced at the California Powder Works facility played a significant role in the development of California's mining industry.

165.

During its operation, the California Powder Works facility employed hundreds of workers, contributing to the local economy.

166.

The construction of the California Powder Works Bridge was a testament to the growing industrialization of Santa Cruz and the need for efficient transportation infrastructure.

167.

The bridge facilitated the movement of raw materials, such as saltpeter and sulfur, to the California Powder Works facility for the production of gunpowder.

168.

The California Powder Works Bridge is listed on the National Register of Historic Places, recognizing its historical significance and architectural value.

169.

Over the years, the California Powder Works Bridge has undergone several renovations and repairs to ensure its structural integrity.

170.

The bridge has withstood floods, earthquakes, and other natural events, demonstrating its resilience and durability.

171.

The California Powder Works Bridge offers scenic views of the San Lorenzo River and the surrounding natural landscape.

172.

The bridge's proximity to the former California Powder Works site adds to its historical context and significance.

173.

The California Powder Works facility ceased operations in the early 20th century, but the bridge remains as a tangible reminder of its industrial past.

174.

The California Powder Works Bridge serves as a popular spot for photography enthusiasts, capturing its unique architecture and historical charm.

175.

The bridge is often included in local walking and cycling routes, providing a picturesque crossing over the San Lorenzo River.

176.

The California Powder Works Bridge has become a symbol of Santa Cruz's rich industrial heritage and commitment to preserving its historical landmarks.

177.

The bridge's restoration efforts have aimed to retain its original character and design, maintaining its historical authenticity.

178.

The California Powder Works Bridge has been featured in various media, including films, documentaries, and books, highlighting its historical significance.

179.

The bridge serves as a connection between the past and the present, reminding residents and visitors of Santa Cruz's industrial roots.

180.

The California Powder Works Bridge is a popular subject for artists, who capture its beauty and historical importance in their works.

181.

The bridge's location within a natural setting attracts nature enthusiasts and wildlife observers, providing opportunities to appreciate the local ecosystem.

182.

The California Powder Works Bridge has become a local landmark and a point of pride for the community.

183.

The bridge's design incorporates elements of both functionality and aesthetics, blending form and function in its construction.

184.

The California Powder Works Bridge is an example of the engineering innovations and techniques employed during the 19th century.

185.

The bridge's preservation and maintenance require ongoing efforts to ensure its continued use and protection.

186.

The California Powder Works Bridge has served as an inspiration for other bridge projects in the region, showcasing the possibilities of combining historical preservation and modern engineering.

187.

The bridge's historical significance has led to its inclusion in educational programs and guided tours, offering visitors insights into its construction and the history of the California Powder Works facility.

188.

The California Powder Works Bridge has been recognized for its contribution to the cultural heritage of Santa Cruz and its importance as a historical landmark.

189.

The bridge's location near parks and recreational areas makes it easily accessible for visitors looking to explore the surrounding natural beauty.

190.

The California Powder Works Bridge serves as a tangible link to Santa Cruz's industrial past and its transformation over time.

191.

The bridge's construction required skilled labor and engineering expertise, reflecting the advancements made in bridge building during the late 19th century.

192.

The California Powder Works Bridge has witnessed significant changes in the landscape and infrastructure of Santa Cruz, providing a sense of continuity in the midst of development.

193.

The bridge's historical significance extends beyond its local context, representing a broader narrative of industrialization and transportation history in California.

194.

The California Powder Works Bridge has become an emblem of Santa Cruz's commitment to preserving its architectural heritage and promoting historical tourism.

195.

The bridge's presence contributes to the overall character and identity of Santa Cruz, adding depth to its cultural landscape.

196.

The California Powder Works Bridge is a popular spot for locals and tourists to pause and appreciate its historical significance while enjoying the natural surroundings.

197.

The bridge's construction materials and techniques reflect the craftsmanship and ingenuity of the time, showcasing the artistry of ironwork and bridge design.

198.

The California Powder Works Bridge has served as a subject of research and study, contributing to the understanding of 19th-century engineering practices.

199.

The bridge's arches and trusses create interesting visual patterns and lines, enhancing its aesthetic appeal.

200.

The California Powder Works Bridge stands as a testament to the vision and ambition of those involved in its construction and the historical legacy it represents.

201.

Cheetahs are the fastest land animals, capable of reaching speeds up to 70 miles per hour (113 kilometers per hour) in short bursts.

202.

They are native to Africa and are found primarily in grasslands and savannas.

203.

Cheetahs have a distinctive coat pattern characterized by black spots on a tawny or golden background, which helps them blend into their environment.

204.

Unlike other big cats, cheetahs have a lean and slender body, adapted for speed and agility.

205.

Cheetahs have a unique anatomy with a flexible spine, oversized nasal passages, and large adrenal glands that contribute to their incredible speed.

206.

They have long, slender legs and non-retractable claws that provide traction while running.

207.

Cheetahs have a specialized respiratory system that allows them to take in more oxygen during their high-speed chases.

208.

They have excellent eyesight, with a wide field of view and a keen ability to spot prey from a distance.

209.

Cheetahs are primarily solitary animals, except for females who raise their cubs together.

210.

They are known for their distinctive hunting strategy, relying on short bursts of speed to chase down and trip their prey.

211.

Cheetahs mainly prey on small to medium-sized ungulates, such as gazelles and impalas.

212.

Cheetahs have a success rate of about 50% in their hunts, with a short burst of energy lasting only about 20-30 seconds.

213.

They have a unique running style called "bounding" where all four feet are momentarily off the ground during each stride.

214.

Cheetahs have excellent acceleration, going from 0 to 60 miles per hour (0 to 97 kilometers per hour) in just a few seconds.

215.

Cheetahs have a relatively small and lightweight body compared to other big cats, weighing between 75 to 140 pounds (34 to 64 kilograms).

216.

They have a high body temperature, around 104 degrees Fahrenheit (40 degrees Celsius), which helps them quickly recover from intense chases.

217.

Cheetahs have a gestation period of about 90 to 95 days, and a female usually gives birth to a litter of three to five cubs.

218.

Cheetah cubs have a unique mantle of fluffy, silvery gray fur on their backs, which provides camouflage and protection in the wild.

219.

Cheetah populations have been declining due to habitat loss, human-wildlife conflict, and illegal hunting.

220.

They are listed as vulnerable by the International Union for Conservation of Nature (IUCN).

221.

Efforts are underway to protect cheetah habitats and establish conservation programs to ensure their survival.

222.

Cheetahs have a variety of vocalizations, including purring, hissing, growling, and chirping.

223.

They have a lifespan of about 10 to 12 years in the wild, but can live up to 20 years in captivity.

224.

Cheetahs have a unique social structure, with males forming small groups called coalitions, typically consisting of brothers from the same litter.

225.

Cheetahs have been admired and depicted in ancient Egyptian artwork and were sometimes kept as pets by pharaohs.

226.

They have large nasal passages that enable them to take in large amounts of oxygen during intense chases.

227.

Cheetahs have sharp, retractable claws that provide traction and grip when running at high speeds.

228.

They have a specialized tail, known as a rudder, which aids in balance and quick turns during hunting.

229.

Cheetahs have a unique tear mark running from the inner corner of their eyes down to the sides of their mouth, which may help reduce glare from the sun and improve their focus while hunting.

230.

They are crepuscular animals, meaning they are most active during dawn and dusk when their prey is also more active.

231.

Cheetahs have a keen sense of hearing and can detect prey or predators from a distance.

232.

They have a relatively small head and jaw compared to other big cats, which allows for a lighter skull and faster movement.

233.

Cheetahs have specialized pads on their feet that provide traction and grip on various terrains.

234.

They can accelerate from 0 to 60 miles per hour (0 to 97 kilometers per hour) faster than most sports cars.

235.

Cheetahs have a unique social behavior called "chirping" or "purring," which is a high-pitched vocalization used for communication among group members.

236.

Cheetahs have a high body temperature that aids in efficient digestion and metabolism.

237.

They have keen eyesight, allowing them to spot potential threats or opportunities from a distance.

238.

Cheetahs have non-retractable claws that provide stability and traction during high-speed chases.

239.

They have a specialized dewclaw, located higher up on their leg, which acts like a rudder during sharp turns while running.

240.

Cheetahs have a flexible spine that allows for an elongated stride and efficient running.

241.

They have a specialized tail that acts as a counterbalance and helps with agility and balance during quick maneuvers.

242.

Cheetahs have a reduced body mass, streamlined body shape, and long legs, which contribute to their exceptional speed.

243.

They have a unique hunting behavior known as "stalk and chase," where they silently approach their prey before launching into a high-speed pursuit.

244.

Cheetahs have been a subject of fascination and inspiration in art, literature, and popular culture for centuries.

245.

They are a flagship species for conservation efforts in Africa, drawing attention to the importance of protecting their habitats and preserving biodiversity.

246.

Cheetahs have a complex social structure, with females being more solitary and males forming small groups called coalitions.

247.

They have specialized adaptations in their eyes, including a large cornea and a reflective layer behind the retina called the tapetum lucidum, which enhances their night vision.

248.

Cheetahs have a unique and intricate communication system, involving vocalizations, body postures, and scent marking.

249.

They have a specialized hunting strategy that relies on stealth and precision, as they need to get close to their prey before initiating the chase.

250.

Cheetahs are remarkable animals that embody grace, speed, and adaptability, making them one of the most iconic and fascinating creatures in the animal kingdom.

251.

Chickaree is another name for the American red squirrel (Tamiasciurus hudsonicus).

252.

They are small-sized squirrels native to North America.

253.

Chickarees are known for their vibrant reddish-brown fur, which helps them blend into their woodland habitats.

254.

They have a distinctive white belly and a bushy tail that often has a black stripe running along its edges.

255.

Chickarees are highly agile and skilled climbers, capable of navigating trees with ease.

256.

They are known for their acrobatic abilities, leaping from branch to branch and performing daring maneuvers.

257.

Chickarees have sharp, curved claws that enable them to grip tree trunks and branches securely.

258.

They are territorial animals and mark their territories using scent glands located on their cheeks.

259.

Chickarees communicate through a variety of vocalizations, including chattering, barking, and trilling sounds.

260.

They have a wide range of diet, consisting of nuts, seeds, cones, mushrooms, berries, and even bird eggs and nestlings.

261.

Chickarees are known for their habit of caching food, storing excess food supplies in various locations for later consumption.

262.

They have excellent memory and can locate their hidden food caches even after an extended period.

263.

Chickarees play a vital role in seed dispersal, as they often forget or fail to retrieve their cached food, allowing seeds to germinate and grow into new plants.

264.

These squirrels are diurnal and are most active during the day, especially in the early morning and late afternoon.

265.

Chickarees are solitary animals, with males and females only coming together for mating.

266.

Males often perform courtship displays to attract females, including chasing and leaping through the trees.

267.

Females give birth to litters of 2-5 young, known as kits, in a nest made of leaves and twigs.

268.

The kits are born blind and hairless, and they rely on their mother's care and milk for the first few weeks of life.

269.

Chickaree kits start venturing out of the nest and exploring their surroundings at around 6-7 weeks old.

270.

The average lifespan of chickarees in the wild is around 5-7 years, although some individuals have been known to live up to 10 years.

271.

They are susceptible to predation by birds of prey, such as hawks and owls, as well as terrestrial predators like foxes and weasels.

272.

Chickarees have adapted to survive in various habitats, including coniferous forests, deciduous forests, and mountainous regions.

273.

They have a wide distribution across North America, ranging from Alaska and Canada to the western and northeastern United States.

274.

Chickarees are agile jumpers, capable of leaping distances of up to 20 feet (6 meters) between trees.

275.

They have sharp incisor teeth that continuously grow throughout their lives, allowing them to gnaw on tree bark, branches, and nuts.

276.

Chickarees have a complex network of tunnels within their territories, providing them with shelter and protection from predators and inclement weather.

277.

They are known for their bold and curious nature, often approaching humans or other animals in search of food.

278.

Chickarees are highly adaptable and can survive in both natural and human-altered environments, including suburban areas and parks.

279.

They are excellent swimmers and can cross bodies of water by paddling their tails and using their hind legs as propellers.

280.

Chickarees are known for their sharp alarm calls, which alert other animals in the vicinity of potential threats.

281.

They are intelligent animals and can quickly learn to navigate complex mazes or solve puzzles to obtain food rewards.

282.

Chickarees have a keen sense of smell, which helps them locate hidden food sources and identify potential predators.

283.

They have a high metabolic rate and need to consume a significant amount of food daily to maintain their energy levels.

284.

Chickarees are known for their territorial disputes with other squirrels, often engaging in loud vocal battles and chasing each other through the treetops.

285.

They are excellent at identifying safe food sources, avoiding toxic or spoiled food items.

286.

Chickarees have adapted to cold climates and grow a thicker coat during the winter months to insulate themselves from the cold.

287.

They are agile problem solvers and can find innovative ways to access hard-to-reach food sources, such as using branches as leverage or using their teeth to chew through obstacles.

288.

Chickarees are known to engage in "mobbing" behavior, where they gather in groups and harass potential predators, such as snakes or birds of prey.

289.

They have a diverse range of vocalizations, including a series of chirps, clicks, and trills, which are used for communication within their social group.

290.

Chickarees have a complex system of scent marking, using glands located on various parts of their body to communicate territorial boundaries and reproductive status.

291.

They have a keen sense of balance and can walk along narrow branches or tree trunks without falling.

292.

Chickarees have large, bushy tails that help them maintain balance while navigating treetops and serve as a visual signal during communication.

293.

They have excellent spatial memory and can recall the locations of food caches, landmarks, and potential threats in their environment.

294.

Chickarees are considered "scatter hoarders" as they store their food in multiple caches rather than a single centralized location.

295.

They are important seed dispersers for many tree species, helping to maintain healthy forest ecosystems.

296.

Chickarees have been observed using deceptive tactics to fool potential predators or competitors, such as feigning injury to distract attention away from their nests or food caches.

297.

They have a highly efficient digestive system that allows them to extract maximum nutrients from their plant-based diet.

298.

Chickarees have sharp senses, including excellent vision, hearing, and touch, which enable them to detect subtle movements or changes in their surroundings.

299.

They have adapted to living in areas prone to forest fires, and their populations can quickly recolonize burned areas, taking advantage of the newly available resources.

300.

Chickarees are charismatic and iconic woodland creatures, playing an essential role in the ecosystems they inhabit and captivating the interest and admiration of nature enthusiasts and researchers alike.

301.

Google was founded in September 1998 by Larry Page and Sergey Brin while they were Ph.D. students at Stanford University.

302.

Originally, Google was a research project called "Backrub" focused on developing a more efficient search engine algorithm.

303.

The name "Google" is a play on the word "googol," which represents the number 1 followed by 100 zeros.

304.

The first Google office was located in a garage in Menlo Park, California, rented from a friend and serving as the company's headquarters.

305.

Google's first significant breakthrough came in 1997 when Page and Brin developed the PageRank algorithm, which revolutionized web search by ranking pages based on their relevance and popularity.

306.

In 1999, Google received its first major investment of $25 million from venture capital firm Sequoia Capital and other investors.

307.

The iconic Google logo was created by Sergey Brin using the free graphics program GIMP.

308.

Google officially incorporated as a company on September 4, 1998, with its headquarters in Mountain View, California.

309.

In 2000, Google became the world's largest search engine, handling more than one billion searches per day.

310.

Google's mission statement is "to organize the world's information and make it universally accessible and useful."

311.

The company's initial public offering (IPO) took place on August 19, 2004, with shares priced at $85. The IPO made many Google employees millionaires overnight.

312.

Google's rapid growth led to the company expanding its services beyond search, including the introduction of Google Images, Google News, and Google Maps.

313.

In 2006, Google acquired YouTube, the popular video-sharing platform, for $1.65 billion.

314.

The company has a culture of innovation and encourages its employees to spend 20% of their work time on projects of their choice, leading to the creation of products like Gmail and Google News.

315.

Google's acquisition of Android Inc. in 2005 marked its entry into the mobile operating system market, ultimately leading to the development of the widely used Android platform.

316.

In 2007, Google launched the Android operating system, which has since become the most widely used mobile operating system globally.

317.

Google's web browser, Google Chrome, was launched in 2008, quickly gaining popularity and becoming one of the most widely used browsers worldwide.

318.

The company's commitment to environmental sustainability is evident through initiatives like carbon neutrality and renewable energy investments.

319.

Google's headquarters in Mountain View, California, is known as the Googleplex and features various amenities for its employees, including free gourmet meals, fitness centers, and recreational facilities.

320.

Google Maps, launched in 2005, revolutionized digital mapping and navigation, providing detailed maps, satellite imagery, and real-time traffic information.

321.

In 2015, Google underwent a corporate restructuring, creating a new parent company called Alphabet Inc., with Google as its subsidiary.

322.

Google is known for its extensive data collection and analysis, using algorithms to provide personalized search results and targeted advertising.

323.

The company has faced criticism and legal challenges regarding user privacy and data protection practices.

324.

Google's philanthropic arm, Google.org, focuses on using technology to address global challenges, including initiatives related to education, health, and environmental sustainability.

325.

Google has a diverse range of products and services, including Google Drive, Google Photos, Google Translate, Google Assistant, and Google Cloud Platform.

326.

The company's annual developer conference, Google I/O, showcases new technologies, features, and updates across its various platforms and services.

327.

Google is known for its playful April Fools' Day pranks, often introducing humorous and imaginative fake products or features.

328.

Google Street View, launched in 2007, provides 360-degree panoramic views of streets around the world, allowing users to explore cities virtually.

329.

In 2011, Google introduced Google+, a social networking platform aimed at competing with Facebook, but it was eventually shut down in 2019.

330.

Google's search engine index is estimated to contain billions of web pages, making it one of the most comprehensive sources of online information.

331.

The company invests heavily in artificial intelligence (AI) research and development, with applications in areas like natural language processing, image recognition, and autonomous driving.

332.

Google has a significant presence in the field of machine learning, with projects such as Google Brain and the development of deep learning algorithms.

333.

Google's "Doodle" is a temporary alteration of the company's logo on its homepage to celebrate notable events, anniversaries, or individuals.

334.

The company operates numerous data centers worldwide to support its online services, utilizing advanced infrastructure and energy-efficient technologies.

335.

Google has a strong commitment to open-source software, contributing to projects like the Linux kernel and releasing various tools and libraries for developers.

336.

The Google Lunar XPRIZE, a competition launched in 2007, aimed to encourage private space exploration, with the ultimate goal of landing a robotic spacecraft on the moon.

337.

In 2017, Google introduced Google Assistant, an AI-powered virtual assistant capable of voice interaction and providing information or performing tasks.

338.

Google's self-driving car project, known as Waymo, aims to develop autonomous vehicles capable of navigating roads without human intervention.

339.

The company's annual "Google Zeitgeist" report provides insights into the year's most popular search queries, reflecting global trends and interests.

340.

Google has a significant presence in the education sector, providing tools like Google Classroom and Google Workspace for educators and students.

341.

The company has made efforts to bridge the digital divide by providing internet connectivity in underserved areas through initiatives like "Project Loon" and "Google Station."

342.

Google has a robust advertising platform known as Google Ads, which allows businesses to reach their target audience through various formats, including search ads, display ads, and video ads.

343.

Google's algorithm updates, such as Panda, Penguin, and Hummingbird, have had significant impacts on search engine optimization (SEO) practices and website rankings.

344.

The company has invested in renewable energy projects, including wind and solar farms, to reduce its environmental footprint and support sustainable energy sources.

345.

Google's cloud computing platform, Google Cloud, offers a range of infrastructure and software services to businesses, including storage, computing, and analytics.

346.

The company actively supports open standards and participates in organizations like the World Wide Web Consortium (W3C) to advance web technologies and interoperability.

347.

Google Translate provides translation services for text, speech, and even images, allowing users to communicate across languages.

348.

Google's annual revenue comes primarily from advertising, with businesses paying for ad placements on its search results pages and other platforms.

349.

The company has made significant acquisitions over the years, including companies like YouTube, DoubleClick, Nest Labs, and Fitbit.

350.

Google continues to innovate and expand its offerings, with ongoing developments in artificial intelligence, virtual reality, augmented reality, and other emerging technologies, shaping the future of digital experiences.

351.

Spotify was founded in April 2006 by Daniel Ek and Martin Lorentzon in Stockholm, Sweden.

352.

The original concept for Spotify came about when Daniel Ek realized the need for a legal and convenient way to access music online.

353.

Spotify's initial name was "Spotifly" but was later changed to "Spotify."

354.

The service was officially launched to the public in October 2008, initially available only in Sweden.

355.

Spotify's early business model faced challenges due to resistance from major record labels, but negotiations eventually led to licensing agreements.

356.

The Spotify logo features a green circle with three curved lines forming an abstract sound wave.

357.

The company introduced a freemium model, allowing users to access a limited version of the service for free with ads or opt for a premium subscription for an ad-free experience.

358.

Spotify's popularity skyrocketed after its international expansion, particularly in Europe and the United States.

359.

The company has continuously expanded its music library, partnering with major record labels and independent artists to offer a wide range of music genres and tracks.

360.

In 2011, Spotify introduced its "Discover Weekly" feature, which curates personalized playlists for users based on their listening habits and preferences.

361.

Spotify went public through a direct listing on the New York Stock Exchange in April 2018.

362.

As of 2021, Spotify has over 345 million monthly active users worldwide, with more than 155 million of them being paid subscribers.

363.

The platform offers a variety of subscription plans, including individual, family, and student options, catering to different user needs.

364.

In addition to music streaming, Spotify has expanded its content offerings to include podcasts, audiobooks, and other audio formats.

365.

Spotify has collaborated with numerous artists and creators to produce exclusive content, including podcasts and live performances.

366.

The company has developed algorithms and machine learning technologies to enhance music recommendations and personalized playlists for users.

367.

Spotify's "Wrapped" feature, introduced in 2015, provides users with personalized insights into their listening habits, top songs, and artists of the year.

368.

In recent years, Spotify has been actively acquiring podcast companies and exclusive podcast content to strengthen its position in the podcasting industry.

369.

Spotify launched its own podcast creation platform called "Anchor" to enable users to create and distribute their podcasts easily.

370.

The company has introduced various social features, allowing users to follow friends, share playlists, and collaborate on collaborative playlists.

371.

Spotify has faced criticism from artists and record labels regarding royalty payments and the overall financial impact of streaming on the music industry.

372.

The platform has implemented various initiatives to support artists, such as Spotify for Artists, which provides tools and analytics to help musicians understand their audience and promote their music.

373.

In 2017, Spotify announced a partnership with the music recognition app Shazam, allowing users to seamlessly identify songs and listen to them on Spotify.

374.

The company has made efforts to expand its services globally, entering new markets and adapting to different languages and cultural preferences.

375.

Spotify's technology infrastructure is built on a complex system of servers and data centers to ensure reliable and scalable music streaming worldwide.

376.

The company has introduced personalized playlists like "Release Radar" and "Daily Mixes" to keep users updated with new releases and tailored music recommendations.

377.

In 2019, Spotify launched its "Your Daily Drive" playlist, combining personalized music and curated podcast content to create a unique audio experience for commuters.

378.

Spotify's annual "Wrapped" campaign has become a highly anticipated event, with users sharing their music statistics and top lists on social media.

379.

The company has collaborated with brands and advertisers to offer targeted ad placements and sponsored playlists.

380.

Spotify has experimented with various innovative features, such as AI-generated playlists like "Discover Weekly" and "Release Radar," and even a music quiz game called "Spotify's Who We Be."

381.

In 2020, Spotify introduced "Group Session," allowing multiple users to control and contribute to a shared playlist in real-time.

382.

The company has launched several initiatives to support emerging artists, such as the Spotify "RADAR" program, which highlights up-and-coming musicians.

383.

Spotify has faced legal challenges and copyright disputes from artists and copyright holders over issues of licensing and royalties.

384.

The company has actively pursued collaborations with other platforms and brands, such as partnering with ride-sharing services like Uber to offer in-car music streaming.

385.

Spotify's acquisition of music data and analytics company The Echo Nest in 2014 has significantly contributed to its music recommendation capabilities.

386.

The company has established relationships with music festivals and live events, offering exclusive content and playlists related to these events.

387.

Spotify has launched various personalized year-in-review campaigns, such as "Wrapped," "Only You," and "Blend," to engage users and celebrate their musical journeys.

388.

In recent years, Spotify has expanded its presence in the podcast industry by acquiring podcast networks like Gimlet Media and Parcast.

389.

The company's "Spotify for Brands" platform offers advertising solutions, allowing brands to reach and engage with Spotify's user base through audio and display ads.

390.

Spotify's technology infrastructure enables users to seamlessly switch between devices and continue listening to music or podcasts without interruption.

391.

The company has developed its own audio streaming codec called "Ogg Vorbis" to deliver high-quality audio while minimizing file size.

392.

Spotify's algorithms analyze user listening patterns, allowing the platform to offer curated playlists like "Discover Weekly" and "Daily Mixes" that cater to individual preferences.

393.

The company has introduced collaborative playlists, enabling users to create and collaborate on shared playlists with friends and family.

394.

Spotify's Discover feature suggests new music and artists based on a user's listening history and preferences, helping users discover new content.

395.

The company has launched various music-centric initiatives, such as the "Spotify Singles" program, where artists record exclusive live performances or cover songs for the platform.

396.

Spotify has developed partnerships with smart speaker manufacturers like Amazon, Google, and Sonos, allowing users to control the app using voice commands.

397.

The company has introduced localized playlists and content, recognizing the importance of regional music and cultural diversity.

398.

Spotify's "Artist Fundraising Pick" feature enables musicians to raise funds directly from their fans by highlighting a chosen cause or project on their profile.

399.

The company's "Spotify Codes" feature allows users to share music and playlists by scanning a unique QR code within the app.

400.

Spotify continues to innovate and expand its offerings, exploring new technologies like voice-controlled music streaming and experimenting with new audio formats to enhance the user experience.

401.

Carmel Mission, officially known as the Mission San Carlos Borromeo del Río Carmelo, is one of the oldest Spanish missions in California, established in 1771.

402.

The mission was founded by Father Junípero Serra, a Franciscan friar who played a significant role in establishing the mission system in California.

403.

Carmel Mission is located in Carmel-by-the-Sea, a picturesque coastal town in Monterey County, California.

404.

The mission was originally built at a different location in Monterey in 1770 but was relocated to its present site in Carmel the following year.

405.

The mission is named after Saint Charles Borromeo, an Italian cardinal and Archbishop of Milan in the 16th century.

406.

The mission's architectural style reflects a combination of Spanish colonial and Moorish influences, featuring a distinctive bell tower and adobe walls.

407.

The interior of the mission includes a beautiful basilica with colorful frescoes, hand-carved wooden statues, and a historic pipe organ.

408.

Carmel Mission was the headquarters of the California mission system and played a significant role in the spread of Christianity among the indigenous people.

409.

The mission was home to a thriving agricultural community, with fields, orchards, and livestock providing sustenance for the residents.

410.

The mission also served as a center for education, with indigenous children being taught various trades and skills by the resident friars.

411.

Carmel Mission was secularized in 1834, following Mexico's independence from Spain, and the land was divided among private owners.

412.

The mission fell into disrepair during the following decades and was even used as a barn at one point.

413.

The mission was restored and renovated in the late 19th century by Harry Downie, an artist and preservationist who recognized its historical and cultural significance.

414.

The mission was designated a National Historic Landmark in 1960, recognizing its importance in American history.

415.

Carmel Mission is still an active parish, serving as a place of worship and spiritual retreat for the local community.

416.

The mission's cemetery is the final resting place of many notable individuals, including some of California's early pioneers and Native American converts.

417.

The mission's gardens are known for their tranquil beauty, featuring native plants, flowers, and fountains.

418.

The mission has a museum that displays a collection of religious artifacts, historic documents, and artwork related to the mission's history.

419.

Carmel Mission has been featured in several movies and TV shows, including the film "Vertigo" directed by Alfred Hitchcock.

420.

The mission hosts various cultural and religious events throughout the year, including concerts, art exhibitions, and religious ceremonies.

421.

Carmel Mission has a rich musical tradition, with a renowned choir that performs during Masses and special events.

422.

The mission's historic cemetery is believed to be the burial site of Father Junípero Serra, although his exact resting place remains uncertain.

423.

The mission has undergone multiple seismic retrofitting projects to ensure its structural integrity and safety.

424.

Carmel Mission has been an inspiration for artists and photographers, with its picturesque architecture and scenic surroundings.

425.

The mission has a gift shop where visitors can purchase religious items, books, and souvenirs related to the mission's history.

426.

The mission's courtyard is a popular spot for visitors to relax and soak in the peaceful ambiance.

427.

Carmel Mission is known for its close ties to the local community, engaging in various outreach programs and charitable activities.

428.

The mission's architecture and historical significance have made it a popular destination for weddings and other special events.

429.

The mission offers guided tours that provide insights into its history, architecture, and religious significance.

430.

The mission's annual Fiesta, held in July, celebrates its founding with live music, traditional dances, food, and entertainment.

431.

The mission's cemetery is believed to be haunted by the spirit of a young girl named Dorotea, whose grave is adorned with fresh flowers.

432.

The mission's bell tower houses several bells, each with a unique tone, used to call the faithful to prayer and mark significant events.

433.

Carmel Mission is surrounded by a serene garden, featuring a collection of roses, citrus trees, and other fragrant plants.

434.

The mission has a rich collection of religious artwork, including paintings, sculptures, and intricate woodwork.

435.

Carmel Mission has been visited by notable figures throughout history, including presidents, dignitaries, and celebrities.

436.

The mission's original water source, a spring known as the Font, still flows to this day and provides water for the mission's gardens.

437.

The mission has a close relationship with the nearby Carmel Mission Basilica School, providing educational opportunities for local students.

438.

Carmel Mission is known for its commitment to environmental sustainability, implementing eco-friendly practices and utilizing solar energy.

439.

The mission hosts regular religious services, including Masses, baptisms, weddings, and funerals, preserving its role as a place of worship.

440.

The mission's historic buildings have been carefully preserved and restored, showcasing the craftsmanship and architectural style of the era.

441.

Carmel Mission has a strong connection to the local Native American communities, working together on cultural preservation and educational initiatives.

442.

The mission has a dedicated team of volunteers who assist with maintaining the grounds, offering tours, and organizing events.

443.

The mission's archives contain a wealth of historical documents, including correspondence, baptismal records, and mission registers.

444.

Carmel Mission is an active participant in interfaith dialogue and hosts events that promote understanding and collaboration among different religious traditions.

445.

The mission's interior features a beautiful collection of Spanish colonial-style furniture, religious artifacts, and decorative elements.

446.

The mission has a deep spiritual significance for many, offering a place for reflection, prayer, and spiritual renewal.

447.

Carmel Mission has been a subject of artistic inspiration for painters, photographers, and writers throughout the years.

448.

The mission's bell tower offers a panoramic view of the surrounding area, including the Pacific Ocean and the picturesque town of Carmel.

449.

The mission's architecture showcases a blend of European and Native American influences, reflecting the cultural exchange that occurred during the mission era.

450.

Carmel Mission continues to serve as a symbol of faith, history, and cultural heritage, attracting visitors from around the world who come to appreciate its beauty and learn about its rich past.

451.

The Carrizo Plain Archeological District is located in San Luis Obispo County, California.

452.

The district encompasses an area of over 13,000 acres and is known for its rich archaeological and cultural significance.

453.

It is home to several Native American tribes, including the Chumash and Yokuts, who have inhabited the area for thousands of years.

454.

The Carrizo Plain Archeological District contains numerous archaeological sites, including village sites, rock art, petroglyphs, and burial grounds.

455.

The district's archaeological sites provide valuable insights into the prehistoric lifestyles, practices, and beliefs of the indigenous people.

456.

The district has evidence of human habitation dating back at least 10,000 years, making it one of the oldest continuously inhabited areas in California.

457.

The Carrizo Plain Archeological District is renowned for its rock art, with numerous rock paintings and petroglyphs depicting various symbols, animals, and human figures.

458.

The rock art found in the district reflects the spiritual and cultural beliefs of the Native American tribes who resided in the area.

459.

The district's archaeological sites have yielded artifacts such as pottery, stone tools, projectile points, and shell beads, providing clues about the material culture of the ancient inhabitants.

460.

The Carrizo Plain Archeological District has been a focus of archaeological research since the early 20th century, with ongoing excavations and studies.

461.

The district is characterized by its unique natural landscape, featuring vast grasslands, rolling hills, and the imposing Caliente Range.

462.

The Carrizo Plain National Monument, which encompasses part of the archeological district, was established in 2001 to protect its natural and cultural resources.

463.

The district's archaeological sites are carefully managed and protected to ensure their preservation for future generations.

464.

The Carrizo Plain Archeological District is an important site for cultural tourism and educational purposes, attracting visitors interested in history and archaeology.

465.

The district's archaeological sites provide a tangible connection to the past, allowing visitors to learn about the indigenous people who lived in the region.

466.

The Carrizo Plain Archeological District is part of the traditional territory of the Chumash people, who continue to maintain a cultural presence in the area.

467.

The district's archaeological sites have contributed to our understanding of the Chumash culture, including their subsistence practices, social organization, and spiritual beliefs.

468.

The Carrizo Plain Archeological District is part of a larger network of archaeological sites and cultural landscapes in Central California.

469.

The district's archaeological significance has been recognized with its inclusion on the National Register of Historic Places.

470.

The Carrizo Plain Archeological District provides opportunities for collaborative research between archaeologists, Native American communities, and academic institutions.

471.

The district's archaeological sites are protected by federal and state laws, which prohibit unauthorized excavation or disturbance.

472.

The Carrizo Plain Archeological District is characterized by its serene and untouched natural environment, allowing visitors to experience the solitude and beauty of the landscape.

473.

The district is home to a diverse range of wildlife, including several endangered and threatened species such as the San Joaquin kit fox and the California condor.

474.

The Carrizo Plain Archeological District has been used as a filming location for movies and documentaries due to its scenic and historic value.

475.

The district's archaeological sites provide opportunities for scientific research, including the study of climate change, human adaptation, and cultural evolution.

476.

The Carrizo Plain Archeological District offers recreational activities such as hiking, wildlife watching, and camping, allowing visitors to explore the natural and cultural wonders of the area.

477.

The district's archaeological sites have been instrumental in establishing the chronology and cultural sequence of prehistoric occupation in Central California.

478.

The Carrizo Plain Archeological District has served as a gathering place and ceremonial center for Native American tribes, where rituals and ceremonies were performed.

479.

The district's archaeological sites have revealed evidence of trade networks and interactions between different Native American groups.

480.

The Carrizo Plain Archeological District is part of a larger effort to preserve and protect California's cultural heritage and promote public awareness of its significance.

481.

The district's archaeological sites contain evidence of the changing landscape over time, including the effects of climate change and human activities.

482.

The Carrizo Plain Archeological District is located within the
traditional territory of the Salinan people, who have a deep cultural
connection to the land.

483.

The district's archaeological sites have been used by Native
American tribes for educational and cultural revitalization purposes.

484.

The Carrizo Plain Archeological District is a testament to the
resilience and adaptability of the indigenous people who thrived in
the region for thousands of years.

485.

The district's archaeological sites provide a glimpse into the daily
lives of the ancient inhabitants, including their food procurement,
shelter construction, and artistic expressions.

486.

The Carrizo Plain Archeological District has witnessed significant
changes in land use over time, from traditional Native American
settlements to Spanish and American colonization.

487.

The district's archaeological sites have been a source of inspiration
for contemporary Native American artists, who draw upon the
cultural heritage and traditions of their ancestors.

488.

The Carrizo Plain Archeological District has been a site of ongoing
collaboration between archaeologists, tribal representatives, and land
management agencies to ensure the preservation and respectful
management of cultural resources.

489.

The district's archaeological sites are an integral part of the cultural landscape, providing a tangible link between the past, present, and future.

490.

The Carrizo Plain Archeological District is located in a region known for its natural beauty and ecological diversity, attracting nature enthusiasts and outdoor enthusiasts.

491.

The district's archaeological sites are a valuable resource for teaching archaeology, anthropology, and Native American studies, offering hands-on learning opportunities for students and researchers.

492.

The Carrizo Plain Archeological District is an important site for the interpretation and dissemination of Native American history and cultural heritage.

493.

The district's archaeological sites have been the subject of public outreach and educational programs, aimed at raising awareness and appreciation for the region's rich cultural heritage.

494.

The Carrizo Plain Archeological District has served as a place of pilgrimage and spiritual significance for Native American communities, who continue to carry out traditional ceremonies and practices in the area.

495.

The district's archaeological sites provide a glimpse into the complex social and political systems of the indigenous people, including their kinship ties, leadership structures, and intergroup relationships.

496.

The Carrizo Plain Archeological District has been a site of archaeological investigations focused on understanding the effects of colonialism and cultural change on the Native American communities.

497.

The district's archaeological sites have yielded evidence of long-distance trade, with artifacts and materials sourced from distant regions.

498.

The Carrizo Plain Archeological District is an example of the ongoing collaboration between archaeologists, tribal representatives, and land management agencies to protect and preserve cultural resources.

499.

The district's archaeological sites are a reminder of the deep connection between the land and the people who have lived on it for thousands of years.

500.

The Carrizo Plain Archeological District is an important heritage site that contributes to our understanding of the diverse cultural history of California and the United States as a whole.

501.

Chickens are domesticated birds that belong to the Gallus gallus domesticus species.

502.

Chickens are descendants of the wild red junglefowl, native to Southeast Asia.

503.

Chickens have been domesticated for thousands of years and were likely first domesticated in ancient China or India.

504.

There are hundreds of different chicken breeds, each with its own unique characteristics and appearances.

505.

Chickens come in various colors and patterns, including black, white, red, brown, and even multicolored feathers.

506.

The average lifespan of a chicken is around 5 to 10 years, but some chickens have been known to live longer.

507.

Chickens are highly social animals and have a hierarchical social structure within their flock.

508.

Chickens communicate with each other through a variety of vocalizations, including clucking, squawking, and crowing.

509.

Chickens are omnivorous animals, meaning they eat both plants and small animals. Their diet consists of grains, seeds, insects, worms, and even small mammals or reptiles.

510.

Chickens have a unique digestive system that allows them to swallow food without chewing it. Instead, they use a muscular organ called the gizzard to grind their food.

511.

Chickens have excellent eyesight and can see a wide range of colors, including ultraviolet light, which humans cannot perceive.

512.

Chickens have a remarkable ability to remember faces and recognize individual humans or animals within their environment.

513.

Chickens are intelligent animals and are capable of problem-solving and learning from their experiences.

514.

Chickens have a natural instinct for dust bathing, which helps keep their feathers clean and free from parasites.

515.

Chickens have a specialized gland near their tail called the uropygial gland, which produces oil to waterproof their feathers.

516.

Chickens have a relatively high body temperature, averaging around 105-107°F (40-42°C).

517.

Chickens have a unique reproductive system. Hens lay eggs regardless of whether they have been fertilized by a rooster. However, a rooster is required for the eggs to develop into chicks.

518.

A rooster's crow is a distinctive sound that serves as a territorial call and a way to communicate with other chickens.

519.

Chickens have a keen sense of hearing and can detect sounds at a wide range of frequencies.

520.

Chickens have excellent peripheral vision, allowing them to detect predators or potential threats from all directions.

521.

Chickens have been bred for various purposes, including meat production, egg-laying, exhibition, and ornamental purposes.

522.

Chickens were first brought to the Americas by European explorers and settlers in the 15th century.

523.

The largest chicken egg ever recorded weighed nearly 12 ounces (340 grams).

524.

Chickens have been used for their therapeutic value in animal-assisted therapy programs, as they are known to reduce stress and provide comfort.

525.

Chickens are capable of recognizing and forming attachments to humans, often bonding with their caretakers.

526.

Chickens have a remarkable sense of direction and can navigate their surroundings, often returning to their coop or roosting spot.

527.

Chickens have a strong maternal instinct, with hens diligently caring for their chicks and teaching them important behaviors.

528.

Chickens have been bred to produce eggs of various colors, including white, brown, blue, green, and even pink.

529.

Chickens have a unique behavior called "tidbitting," where they make a special clucking sound to attract the attention of other chickens and share food discoveries.

530.

Chickens have been found to possess numerical abilities and can discriminate between different quantities.

531.

Chickens have a wide range of vocalizations, including specific calls to alert other chickens of danger or to communicate food discoveries.

532.

Chickens have excellent balance and coordination, allowing them to navigate various terrains and even roost on high perches.

533.

Chickens have been used in scientific research to study genetics, behavior, and diseases due to their biological similarities to humans.

534.

Chickens have been used for centuries in religious and cultural ceremonies and symbolize various meanings in different cultures.

535.

Chickens have a strong sense of self-preservation and will instinctively flee or hide from potential threats.

536.

Chickens have been known to exhibit problem-solving skills, such as learning to open latches or access food sources.

537.

Chickens have a unique ability to sunbathe, stretching out their wings and exposing their feathers to sunlight to absorb vitamin D.

538.

Chickens have a remarkable sense of balance and can perch on narrow surfaces or even walk on tightropes.

539.

Chickens have been bred for specific traits, such as feather color, body size, or specific comb shapes.

540.

Chickens have a diverse range of vocalizations, including purring, clucking, cackling, and even growling.

541.

Chickens have a natural instinct for scratching the ground, which helps them uncover insects, seeds, and other food sources.

542.

Chickens have a unique defense mechanism called "puffing up," where they fluff their feathers to appear larger and more intimidating to potential predators.

543.

Chickens have a keen sense of smell and can detect scents in their environment.

544.

Chickens have been used for their manure as a valuable fertilizer for agricultural purposes.

545.

Chickens have been depicted in various forms of art, literature, and folklore throughout history.

546.

Chickens have a distinctive "pecking order" within their flock, establishing a hierarchy based on dominance.

547.

Chickens have a remarkable ability to adapt to various climates and environments, which is why they are found in different parts of the world.

548.

Chickens have been found to possess basic problem-solving skills, such as learning to navigate mazes or access rewards.

549.

Chickens have a specialized adaptation called the crop, which is an enlarged pouch-like structure in their digestive system that stores and softens food before digestion.

550.

Chickens have played an important role in sustainable farming practices, as they can help control pests, provide organic fertilizers, and contribute to a diverse ecosystem.

551.

Chimpanzees are one of the closest living relatives to humans, sharing about 98% of our DNA.

552.

They are native to the forests and woodlands of Central and West Africa.

553.

Chimpanzees are highly intelligent animals and have shown remarkable problem-solving abilities.

554.

They live in complex social groups called communities, consisting of multiple males, females, and their offspring.

555.

Chimpanzees have a diverse diet that includes fruits, leaves, seeds, insects, and even small mammals.

556.

They have been observed using tools, such as sticks or rocks, to gather food or extract termites from their mounds.

557.

Chimpanzees have excellent memory and can remember the location of food sources and other important landmarks.

558.

They communicate using a variety of vocalizations, gestures, and facial expressions.

559.

Chimpanzees have been known to engage in elaborate grooming rituals, which help build social bonds within their community.

560.

They exhibit a wide range of emotions, including joy, sadness, anger, and fear.

561.

Chimpanzees have a complex social structure with dominant individuals and hierarchical relationships.

562.

They display different behaviors, such as hugging, kissing, holding hands, and patting backs, to show affection.

563.

Chimpanzees have been observed using teamwork to achieve certain goals, such as hunting or defending their territory.

564.

They have the ability to recognize themselves in a mirror, indicating a level of self-awareness.

565.

Chimpanzees are excellent climbers and spend a significant amount of time in trees.

566.

They have opposable thumbs and can manipulate objects with precision.

567.

Chimpanzees have been observed using leaves as makeshift umbrellas or sponges to collect water.

568.

They have a lifespan of around 40 to 50 years in the wild, although some individuals have been known to live longer.

569.

Chimpanzees have a strong maternal bond, and mothers are highly protective of their offspring.

570.

They can learn and acquire new behaviors through observation and imitation.

571.

Chimpanzees have been known to engage in territorial disputes and can be aggressive towards other communities.

572.

They exhibit a wide range of facial expressions, including smiles, frowns, and even laughter-like sounds.

573.

Chimpanzees have been observed using leaves as blankets or cushions for more comfortable resting.

574.

They have a complex vocal repertoire, including various calls, screams, and pant-hoots used for communication.

575.

Chimpanzees have a highly adaptable diet, allowing them to survive in a variety of habitats.

576.

They have been found to engage in play behavior, which helps them develop social skills and problem-solving abilities.

577.

Chimpanzees have a strong sense of empathy and have been observed comforting distressed individuals.

578.

They can recognize and remember individual faces within their community.

579.

Chimpanzees have been observed using rocks as weapons, throwing them at potential threats or rivals.

580.

They have a keen sense of hearing and can detect a wide range of sounds, including distant calls or alarms.

581.

Chimpanzees have been studied extensively to gain insights into human evolution, behavior, and cognition.

582.

They exhibit a form of communication called "chimp kissing," where they press their lips together in a social bonding gesture.

583.

Chimpanzees have been shown to exhibit cultural differences within different communities, such as using different tools or displaying unique behaviors.

584.

They have a high level of curiosity and explore their surroundings to gather information about their environment.

585.

Chimpanzees have been observed using leaves as makeshift toilet paper or for hygiene purposes.

586.

They have been known to exhibit altruistic behavior, helping injured or disabled individuals within their group.

587.

Chimpanzees have a complex mating system, with females usually mating with multiple males within their community.

588.

They have been observed engaging in elaborate courtship displays, including vocalizations and physical gestures.

589.

Chimpanzees have a well-developed sense of smell, which they use to detect ripe fruits or potential predators.

590.

They have a strong sense of territoriality and use vocalizations and displays to mark their boundaries.

591.

Chimpanzees have been studied for their ability to solve puzzles and complex cognitive tasks.

592.

They have been shown to have a concept of time, being able to anticipate future events or remember past experiences.

593.

Chimpanzees exhibit a form of cultural transmission, passing on learned behaviors from one generation to another.

594.

They have been observed using leaves as makeshift fans to cool themselves during hot weather.

595.

Chimpanzees have been known to engage in "rain dances," where they stand upright and display excited behaviors during rainfall.

596.

They have a sophisticated system of communication, including gestural signals and body postures.

597.

Chimpanzees have a highly flexible diet and can adapt to seasonal variations in food availability.

598.

They have been observed using different types of vocalizations to communicate specific messages, such as alarm calls or food calls.

599.

Chimpanzees have a strong sense of individuality and exhibit personal preferences and unique personalities.

600.

They are considered an endangered species due to habitat loss, poaching, and disease, and conservation efforts are underway to protect their populations.

601.

Trader Joe's was founded in 1958 by Joe Coulombe in Pasadena, California.

602.

The original name of the store was "Pronto Market," but it was later changed to "Trader Joe's" to evoke a South Seas tropical theme.

603.

The store's unique nautical theme, including the captain's hat-wearing employees, was inspired by Coulombe's love for travel and exploration.

604.

Trader Joe's initially catered to young, budget-conscious customers by offering discounted groceries and specialty items.

605.

The store introduced its own private label products in the 1970s, focusing on high-quality, affordable, and unique offerings.

606.

Trader Joe's was one of the first grocery stores to introduce a "no artificial preservatives, flavors, or colors" policy for its private label products.

607.

The company became employee-owned in 1979 through an employee stock ownership plan (ESOP), which helped foster a strong company culture and commitment to customer service.

608.

In the 1980s, Trader Joe's started expanding beyond California, opening stores in other states such as Arizona and Nevada.

609.

The store's focus on exotic and international foods began to take shape in the 1990s, with the introduction of unique products from around the world.

610.

Trader Joe's became known for its fun and quirky store features, including hand-painted signs, whimsical product labels, and staff wearing Hawaiian shirts.

611.

The "Fearless Flyer," Trader Joe's iconic newsletter, was first introduced in the 1990s and continues to provide customers with information on new products and store news.

612.

The store's commitment to sustainability and eco-friendly practices is evident in its efforts to reduce packaging waste and source environmentally responsible products.

613.

Trader Joe's has a strong focus on customer satisfaction, offering a generous return policy and a commitment to quality and freshness.

614.

The company is known for fostering a positive work environment, providing employees with competitive wages, benefits, and opportunities for advancement.

615.

Trader Joe's has developed a loyal customer base that appreciates the store's unique products, reasonable prices, and enjoyable shopping experience.

616.

The store's expansion continued into the 2000s, reaching the East Coast and expanding internationally to countries like Canada and the United Kingdom.

617.

Trader Joe's has won numerous awards and accolades for its products, including recognition for its wine selection and innovative food offerings.

618.

The company has a strong commitment to giving back to the community and has partnered with various organizations to support hunger relief, education, and environmental initiatives.

619.

Trader Joe's has a policy of donating unsold food items to local food banks and charities, reducing food waste and helping those in need.

620.

The store's "Two-Buck Chuck," a line of affordable wines, gained popularity for its quality and value.

621.

Trader Joe's has a dedicated following on social media, with customers sharing their favorite products and recipes under hashtags like #TraderJoesFinds.

622.

The company is known for its unique seasonal products, such as pumpkin-flavored treats during the fall and peppermint-themed goodies during the holidays.

623.

Trader Joe's sources its products directly from suppliers, often working with small and independent producers to offer unique and artisanal offerings.

624.

The store's Hawaiian shirt-wearing employees are known for their friendly and helpful customer service, contributing to the store's inviting atmosphere.

625.

Trader Joe's is committed to diversity and inclusivity, with a focus on hiring a diverse workforce and offering products that cater to different dietary needs and preferences.

626.

The store's pricing strategy emphasizes value for money, offering high-quality products at competitive prices.

627.

Trader Joe's has a strong emphasis on product quality, conducting rigorous taste tests and quality checks before stocking items on its shelves.

628.

The company has been praised for its transparency in labeling, providing detailed ingredient lists and clear allergen information on its products.

629.

Trader Joe's regularly introduces new and innovative products to its stores, often responding to customer feedback and trends in the food industry.

630.

The company has a commitment to animal welfare and offers a range of vegetarian and vegan options to cater to different dietary choices.

631.

Trader Joe's has a strong online presence, with a website that provides information on products, recipes, and store locations.

632.

The store's checkout process is known for its speed and efficiency, with dedicated employees working to ensure a smooth and hassle-free experience for customers.

633.

Trader Joe's has a policy of avoiding excessive advertising and marketing, relying instead on word-of-mouth recommendations and customer loyalty.

634.

The company values simplicity in its store layout and product selection, focusing on offering a curated range of high-quality items rather than overwhelming customers with choice.

635.

Trader Joe's has been recognized as a leader in the grocery industry, receiving awards for its customer service, employee satisfaction, and ethical business practices.

636.

The company actively seeks customer feedback and suggestions, often incorporating customer ideas into new product developments or store improvements.

637.

Trader Joe's has a strong commitment to food safety and follows strict protocols to ensure the quality and freshness of its products.

638.

The store's "endless aisle" approach allows customers to request specific products that may not be available on the shelves, providing a personalized shopping experience.

639.

Trader Joe's regularly collaborates with local businesses and organizations to offer exclusive products and support the local community.

640.

The store has a unique selection of pantry staples, including a wide range of spices, sauces, and condiments from various cuisines around the world.

641.

Trader Joe's has a focus on reducing plastic waste, offering reusable bags and encouraging customers to bring their own containers for bulk items.

642.

The company has a commitment to fair trade practices, partnering with organizations that support sustainable farming and ethical sourcing.

643.

Trader Joe's has a diverse range of frozen food options, including vegetarian and vegan meals, convenient snacks, and globally inspired dishes.

644.

The company has a commitment to minimizing food additives, preservatives, and artificial ingredients in its products, focusing on natural and wholesome offerings.

645.

Trader Joe's has a loyal customer base that appreciates the store's unique product offerings, affordable prices, and enjoyable shopping experience.

646.

The company regularly introduces new and limited-edition items, keeping customers excited and engaged with new flavors and seasonal specialties.

647.

Trader Joe's has a strong presence in the online community, with blogs and social media accounts dedicated to sharing customer favorites and creative recipes.

648.

The store's "fearless flyer" newsletter often features informative articles about ingredients, cooking tips, and product spotlights.

649.

Trader Joe's has a commitment to reducing food waste, working with local farmers to repurpose imperfect or surplus produce into delicious and affordable products.

650.

The company continues to innovate and evolve, staying true to its mission of providing customers with high-quality, unique, and affordable products in a friendly and enjoyable shopping environment.

651.

Zoom was founded in 2011 by Eric Yuan, a former executive at the video conferencing company WebEx.

652.

The original name of the company was "Saasbee Inc.," but it was later changed to Zoom Video Communications.

653.

Eric Yuan came up with the idea for Zoom after experiencing frustration with the existing video conferencing solutions and wanting to create a simpler and more user-friendly platform.

654.

Zoom was officially launched in 2013 and quickly gained popularity for its ease of use, high-quality video, and robust features.

655.

The company's mission is to make video communications frictionless and reliable, enabling people to connect and collaborate seamlessly.

656.

In its early years, Zoom primarily focused on serving the enterprise market, providing video conferencing solutions for businesses and organizations.

657.

Zoom's breakthrough moment came in 2020 during the COVID-19 pandemic when the demand for remote work and online meetings skyrocketed.

658.

The company experienced exponential growth during this time, becoming a household name and one of the most widely used video conferencing platforms.

659.

Zoom's user base expanded rapidly, from primarily business users to individuals, families, and even educational institutions using it for online classes.

660.

Zoom's user-friendly interface and intuitive features, such as virtual backgrounds and screen sharing, contributed to its widespread adoption.

661.

The term "Zoom" became synonymous with online meetings, with people using the term generically to refer to any video conferencing session.

662.

Zoom's cloud-based infrastructure allowed for seamless scalability, enabling it to handle the massive increase in user traffic during the pandemic.

663.

The company introduced several security enhancements and encryption features to address privacy concerns and ensure the safety of user data.

664.

Zoom became a publicly traded company in April 2019, listing its shares on the NASDAQ stock exchange under the ticker symbol "ZM."

665.

Zoom's success in the stock market made Eric Yuan a billionaire, and he was named the Businessperson of the Year by Time magazine in 2020.

666.

Zoom's revenue grew significantly in 2020, with the company reporting a year-over-year revenue increase of over 300%.

667.

Zoom's success led to various partnerships and integrations with other tech companies and platforms, expanding its functionalities and user reach.

668.

The company introduced Zoom Rooms, a solution for setting up video conference rooms with dedicated hardware and software.

669.

Zoom has been praised for its accessibility features, including support for closed captioning, screen readers, and keyboard shortcuts, making it inclusive for users with disabilities.

670.

In 2020, Zoom launched the "Zoom for Home" product line, offering dedicated video conferencing devices for remote workers.

671.

Zoom has faced security and privacy challenges during its rapid growth, prompting the company to strengthen its security measures and release regular updates.

672.

The company invested in research and development to improve the platform's performance and introduce new features like breakout rooms and webinar capabilities.

673.

Zoom's success led to an increase in competition, with other tech giants introducing their own video conferencing solutions to compete in the market.

674.

Zoom's popularity extended beyond business meetings, with people using it for virtual happy hours, online events, and even virtual weddings.

675.

The company actively engages with its user community, hosting virtual events and webinars to provide training and support.

676.

Zoom has been recognized with numerous awards and accolades, including being named a leader in the Gartner Magic Quadrant for Meeting Solutions.

677.

The company's cultural impact was significant, with the term "Zoom fatigue" being coined to describe the exhaustion from excessive video conferencing.

678.

Zoom's success and widespread usage led to its inclusion in popular culture, with references and parodies in TV shows, movies, and social media.

679.

Zoom's platform expanded beyond video conferencing, offering additional features like instant messaging, file sharing, and cloud storage.

680.

The company's mobile app gained popularity, allowing users to join meetings and collaborate on the go using their smartphones or tablets.

681.

Zoom introduced features specifically designed for educational institutions, enabling virtual classrooms and remote learning.

682.

The company launched Zoom Phone, a cloud-based phone system that integrates with the video conferencing platform.

683.

Zoom's philanthropic efforts included providing free accounts to schools during the pandemic and donating to various charitable organizations.

684.

Zoom's success resulted in a significant increase in its workforce, with the company hiring thousands of new employees to support its growing user base.

685.

The company actively sought user feedback and incorporated customer suggestions into product updates and improvements.

686.

Zoom's user interface underwent several redesigns to enhance usability and improve the overall user experience.

687.

Zoom's virtual backgrounds feature became a hit, allowing users to customize their video backgrounds and add a touch of fun to their meetings.

688.

The company actively pursued partnerships with healthcare organizations, offering telehealth solutions and facilitating remote patient consultations.

689.

Zoom played a crucial role in maintaining social connections during periods of lockdown and physical distancing, helping people stay connected with friends and family.

690.

The company expanded its services beyond video conferencing, offering webinars, virtual events, and live streaming capabilities.

691.

Zoom's customer support team grew in size to handle the increased demand for assistance, providing timely responses and troubleshooting guidance.

692.

The company's commitment to sustainability included efforts to reduce its carbon footprint and promote eco-friendly practices.

693.

Zoom launched the "Zoomtopia" conference, an annual event where users, developers, and industry experts gather to learn about the latest innovations and share best practices.

694.

The company invested in artificial intelligence and machine learning technologies to enhance meeting experiences and improve video and audio quality.

695.

Zoom's success led to an increase in job opportunities within the remote work and video conferencing sectors, contributing to job creation.

696.

The company expanded its global presence, establishing offices and data centers in various countries to better serve its international user base.

697.

Zoom's virtual backgrounds feature became a creative outlet for users, with people using it for virtual parties, themed events, and showcasing their personality.

698.

The company actively engaged with educators and schools, offering resources and training to optimize the use of Zoom for remote learning.

699.

Zoom's platform supported various types of meetings, from one-on-one conversations to large-scale conferences with thousands of participants.

700.

The company's continuous innovation and commitment to user satisfaction positioned Zoom as a leading video conferencing solution, transforming the way people communicate and collaborate globally.

701.

Chicano Park is located in the Barrio Logan neighborhood of San Diego, California.

702.

The park covers a 7.4-acre area beneath the San Diego-Coronado Bridge.

703.

Chicano Park was established on April 22, 1970, as a result of a community-led occupation of the land.

704.

The park is known for its vibrant and colorful murals, which depict various aspects of Chicano history, culture, and social justice movements.

705.

There are over 80 murals in Chicano Park, making it the largest collection of outdoor murals in the United States.

706.

The murals in Chicano Park tell stories of activism, civil rights, cultural pride, and resistance.

707.

The park serves as a cultural and political gathering place for the Chicano community and other social justice movements.

708.

Chicano Park was listed on the National Register of Historic Places in 2013.

709.

The park is recognized as a California Historical Landmark and a National Historic Landmark.

710.

The Chicano Park Steering Committee was formed in 1970 to advocate for the park's creation and preservation.

711.

The park is home to the Chicano Park Museum and Cultural Center, which provides educational programs and exhibits about Chicano history and culture.

712.

Chicano Park hosts various cultural events and celebrations throughout the year, including the annual Chicano Park Day festival.

713.

The park is an important symbol of resistance against social and environmental injustices faced by the Chicano community.

714.

Chicano Park serves as a hub for community organizing and activism.

715.

The park was established on land that was originally promised to the community as a recreational space but was instead designated for a California Highway Patrol substation.

716.

The occupation of the land and subsequent establishment of the park were driven by community members demanding self-determination and cultural representation.

717.

The park's iconic Aztec-inspired sculptures and symbols reflect the Indigenous heritage and ancestry of the Chicano community.

718.

Chicano Park's murals have been created by numerous artists over the years, including renowned muralists such as Salvador Torres, Victor Ochoa, and Mario Torero.

719.

The imagery in the murals often highlights social and political issues affecting the Chicano community, such as immigration, labor rights, and police brutality.

720.

Chicano Park has become a symbol of grassroots activism and the power of community mobilization.

721.

The park has inspired similar community-driven mural projects and parks across the United States and internationally.

722.

The annual Chicano Park Day festival attracts thousands of visitors, showcasing live music, traditional dance performances, food vendors, and cultural exhibits.

723.

The park is a testament to the resilience and cultural pride of the Chicano community in the face of marginalization and discrimination.

724.

Chicano Park has been featured in various documentaries, books, and academic studies as a significant site of cultural and historical importance.

725.

The murals in Chicano Park are created using a combination of spray paint, acrylics, and other artistic mediums.

726.

Many of the murals have been restored and maintained by artists and community volunteers to preserve their historical and artistic value.

727.

The park's location beneath the San Diego-Coronado Bridge adds to its distinctive atmosphere and visual appeal.

728.

Chicano Park has become a popular destination for tourists, art enthusiasts, and those interested in learning about Chicano history and culture.

729.

The park's murals have served as backdrops for music videos, fashion shoots, and other artistic endeavors.

730.

Chicano Park has been a site for protests and rallies advocating for social justice causes beyond the Chicano community, including LGBTQ+ rights, environmental justice, and indigenous rights.

731.

The park is often used as an outdoor classroom, providing educational opportunities for students to learn about art, history, and social movements.

732.

Chicano Park has been a focal point for Chicano artists to express their creativity and share their cultural heritage with a wider audience.

733.

The park's murals are known for their vibrant colors, intricate details, and powerful symbolism.

734.

Chicano Park has received numerous awards and accolades for its cultural significance and community impact.

735.

The park has been featured in mainstream media, including television shows, movies, and music videos.

736.

Chicano Park has become an important gathering place for intergenerational dialogue and the passing down of cultural traditions.

737.

The park's murals often feature iconic figures from Chicano history, such as Cesar Chavez, Dolores Huerta, and Emiliano Zapata.

738.

Chicano Park's murals incorporate elements of both Mexican and American cultural identities, reflecting the bicultural experience of the Chicano community.

739.

The park's iconic "Welcome to Chicano Park" sign, located at the entrance, has become an emblematic symbol of the park's identity and significance.

740.

Chicano Park has been recognized as a space that fosters healing, resilience, and empowerment for individuals and the community as a whole.

741.

The park's murals are constantly evolving, with new artwork being added and older murals being restored or refreshed.

742.

Chicano Park's murals have inspired social and political conversations, sparking dialogue about identity, history, and social justice.

743.

The park has been a site for cultural performances, including traditional dance, music, and theatrical productions.

744.

Chicano Park serves as a reminder of the ongoing struggle for social and cultural justice faced by marginalized communities.

745.

The park's murals often depict the diversity of the Chicano community, representing different regions, ethnic backgrounds, and historical experiences.

746.

Chicano Park has become a source of pride and inspiration for the broader Latino community, as well as other marginalized groups.

747.

The park's murals have influenced the Chicano art movement, contributing to the development of a distinct Chicano visual language and aesthetic.

748.

Chicano Park has served as a venue for community meetings, workshops, and cultural exchange programs.

749.

The park has been featured in cultural festivals and events celebrating the diversity and richness of the San Diego community.

750.

Chicano Park stands as a living testament to the power of art, community, and collective action in preserving cultural heritage and promoting social change.

751.

Coloma is a small town located in El Dorado County, California.

752.

The town is situated in the Sierra Nevada foothills, along the banks of the South Fork American River.

753.

Coloma is most famous for being the site of the California Gold Rush discovery in 1848.

754.

The discovery of gold in Coloma by James W. Marshall on January 24, 1848, sparked the largest mass migration in American history.

755.

The gold discovery at Sutter's Mill, located in Coloma, led to the rapid development of the state of California.

756.

Coloma was originally inhabited by the Nisenan and Maidu Native American tribes.

757.

The town was named after the original Native American name for the area, "Cullumah," meaning "beautiful."

758.

Coloma was the site of California's first significant gold rush settlement.

759.

The town quickly grew in population as thousands of gold prospectors arrived, seeking their fortunes.

760.

The historic Marshall Gold Discovery State Historic Park preserves the site where gold was first discovered in Coloma.

761.

The park features a replica of Sutter's Mill and a museum that showcases artifacts from the gold rush era.

762.

Coloma was the birthplace of the California gold mining industry, which had a significant impact on the economic and cultural development of the region.

763.

The Gold Rush brought people from all over the world to Coloma, creating a diverse and multicultural community.

764.

Many famous and influential figures, such as John Sutter and James W. Marshall, were associated with the history of Coloma.

765.

Coloma became a center for trade, commerce, and transportation during the Gold Rush era.

766.

The town had a vibrant economy with numerous businesses, including saloons, stores, hotels, and blacksmith shops.

767.

The Coloma Road, also known as the "Emigrant Trail," became one of the main routes for settlers traveling to California during the Gold Rush.

768.

The town's population declined after the initial gold rush period as prospectors moved on to other areas in search of gold.

769.

Coloma experienced a revival in the 20th century as the site of the Marshall Gold Discovery State Historic Park, attracting tourists and history enthusiasts.

770.

Today, Coloma is a popular tourist destination, offering visitors a chance to experience the history of the Gold Rush era.

771.

The town retains its historic charm with buildings, artifacts, and monuments from the 19th century.

772.

Coloma is surrounded by scenic natural beauty, including the American River, rolling hills, and oak woodlands.

773.

The area offers opportunities for outdoor activities such as hiking, camping, fishing, and whitewater rafting.

774.

The Coloma-Lotus Valley is known for its rich biodiversity, with diverse plant and animal species.

775.

The town hosts annual events and festivals, such as the Gold Discovery Day celebration, where visitors can witness reenactments of the gold discovery.

776.

Coloma was designated as a California Historical Landmark in 1950.

777.

The historic Gold Rush era buildings in Coloma showcase architectural styles of the time, including rustic cabins and Victorian structures.

778.

The Coloma Schoolhouse, built-in 1872, is one of the oldest one-room schoolhouses still standing in California.

779.

The Coloma Cemetery is the final resting place for many early settlers and gold rush pioneers.

780.

Coloma's location on the South Fork American River makes it a popular spot for recreational gold panning.

781.

The area surrounding Coloma is renowned for its wineries, offering wine tasting experiences for visitors.

782.

Coloma has been the setting for several movies and television shows depicting the California Gold Rush era.

783.

The town's scenic beauty and historical significance make it a popular destination for artists and photographers.

784.

Coloma has a mild Mediterranean climate, with hot summers and mild winters, making it an ideal place for outdoor activities year-round.

785.

The South Fork American River, flowing through Coloma, is a popular destination for whitewater rafting and kayaking.

786.

Coloma is part of the El Dorado Wine Region, known for its production of award-winning wines.

787.

The town is home to several vineyards and wineries, offering wine tours and tastings.

788.

Coloma is surrounded by numerous state and regional parks, providing opportunities for hiking, camping, and wildlife observation.

789.

The Coloma Valley was once home to a diverse ecosystem, including grizzly bears, elk, and other native wildlife.

790.

The area is rich in geological formations, with exposed rock formations, granite outcroppings, and scenic vistas.

791.

Coloma is a gateway to the Sierra Nevada Mountains, offering access to outdoor activities such as hiking, skiing, and mountain biking.

792.

The town has preserved its historic character and small-town charm, with quaint shops, restaurants, and bed and breakfast accommodations.

793.

The Coloma Valley is known for its wildflower displays in the spring, with vibrant colors and a variety of species.

794.

Coloma has several hiking trails, including the South Fork American River Trail, providing scenic views of the river and surrounding landscape.

795.

The area is home to a diverse bird population, making it a popular destination for birdwatching enthusiasts.

796.

Coloma is located near the Eldorado National Forest, offering opportunities for camping, fishing, and nature exploration.

797.

The town has a rich Native American heritage, with archaeological sites and artifacts dating back thousands of years.

798.

The Coloma area is known for its gold mining history, and visitors can still try their hand at gold panning in designated areas.

799.

The town hosts historical reenactments and living history events, allowing visitors to step back in time and experience the Gold Rush era.

800.

Coloma is a place of historical significance, natural beauty, and outdoor recreation, making it a memorable destination for visitors interested in California's Gold Rush history.

801.

Chinchillas are small rodents native to the Andes Mountains in South America, specifically in Bolivia, Chile, Peru, and Argentina.

802.

They are known for their soft and dense fur, which is considered one of the softest and most luxurious in the world.

803.

Chinchillas have a lifespan of around 10-20 years, making them relatively long-lived for small mammals.

804.

Chinchillas are crepuscular, which means they are most active during dawn and dusk.

805.

In the wild, chinchillas live in burrows or rock crevices to protect themselves from predators and extreme temperatures.

806.

Chinchillas have large, round ears that help them detect sounds and predators in their environment.

807.

They have a keen sense of hearing and can communicate through a range of vocalizations, including chirps, barks, and purring sounds.

808.

Chinchillas have long hind limbs, which make them excellent jumpers and allow them to escape from predators.

809.

They are herbivores and primarily feed on grasses, leaves, seeds, and bark in their natural habitat.

810.

Chinchillas have specialized teeth that continuously grow throughout their lives, requiring them to chew on hard objects to wear them down.

811.

Chinchillas are social animals and often live in colonies or family groups in the wild.

812.

They have a unique dust bathing behavior to keep their fur clean and maintain its natural oils.

813.

Chinchillas have a thick fur coat that provides excellent insulation against cold temperatures in their native mountainous habitat.

814.

The fur of chinchillas comes in a variety of colors, including gray, beige, white, and black, with different coat patterns and markings.

815.

Chinchillas are agile climbers and can navigate rocky terrain with ease.

816.

They have long, bushy tails that help them maintain balance while climbing and jumping.

817.

Chinchillas have large eyes positioned on the sides of their head, giving them a wide field of vision to detect predators.

818.

Chinchillas are known for their unique behavior called "fur slip," where they can release a patch of fur to escape from the grasp of predators.

819.

In the wild, chinchillas may hibernate during periods of extreme cold or food scarcity.

820.

Chinchillas are popular pets known for their playful and curious nature.

821.

They require specialized care, including a dust bath, a proper diet, and a spacious cage with opportunities for exercise.

822.

Chinchillas have dense fur that allows them to float on water, making them excellent swimmers if necessary.

823.

Chinchillas have a sensitive respiratory system and are susceptible to respiratory infections, so they should be kept in a clean and dust-free environment.

824.

They are nocturnal animals, meaning they are most active during the night and sleep during the day.

825.

Chinchillas have a unique ability to jump up to six feet in the air.

826.

They have a well-developed sense of touch, with sensitive whiskers and tactile pads on their paws.

827.

Chinchillas have a gestation period of around 111 days, and females typically give birth to one or two babies called "kits."

828.

Baby chinchillas are born fully furred and with their eyes open, and they can start eating solid food within a few weeks.

829.

Chinchillas have a friendly and sociable nature, but they may take time to bond with their owners and establish trust.

830.

Chinchillas have a delicate digestive system and should be provided with a diet rich in fiber to prevent digestive issues.

831.

Chinchillas are agile jumpers and climbers, so their cages should be equipped with platforms, ramps, and toys to keep them active and engaged.

832.

They are sensitive to high temperatures and can easily overheat, so they should be kept in a cool and well-ventilated environment.

833.

Chinchillas have a natural instinct for digging, so providing them with a suitable digging area or a dust bath helps satisfy their natural behavior.

834.

Chinchillas are known for their fastidious grooming habits and spend a significant amount of time cleaning their fur.

835.

They have a unique ability to rotate their ears independently, allowing them to locate sounds accurately.

836.

Chinchillas have a strong bite force due to their large incisors, which they use for chewing and gnawing on objects.

837.

They have a sensitive bladder and should have access to fresh water at all times to prevent dehydration.

838.

Chinchillas have a thick, leathery pad on the soles of their feet, providing them with good traction and preventing them from slipping.

839.

They have a unique digestive system called hindgut fermentation, which helps break down plant materials and extract nutrients.

840.

Chinchillas have a natural propensity for exploring and may exhibit curious behavior when provided with a stimulating environment.

841.

They are known for their vocal repertoire, which includes chirping, barking, growling, and purring sounds to communicate with other chinchillas.

842.

Chinchillas have a keen sense of smell and use scent marking to communicate territorial boundaries and reproductive status.

843.

They are highly adaptable animals and can adjust to various altitudes and environmental conditions.

844.

Chinchillas have been extensively hunted for their fur, leading to a significant decline in their population in the wild.

845.

Efforts have been made to conserve chinchillas through captive breeding programs and protected reserves.

846.

Chinchillas are considered a vulnerable species and are listed on the International Union for Conservation of Nature (IUCN) Red List.

847.

The trade of wild chinchillas and their fur is regulated to protect their population and prevent illegal poaching.

848.

Chinchillas are excellent jumpers, capable of leaping distances of up to five feet.

849.

Chinchillas have sharp claws that allow them to grip onto various surfaces and climb with ease.

850.

Chinchillas are fascinating creatures with unique adaptations, making them a beloved choice for both pet owners and wildlife enthusiasts.

851.

Chinese hamsters, also known as striped hamsters or dwarf hamsters, are small rodents native to northern China and Mongolia.

852.

They have a slender body shape, measuring around 3-4 inches in length, with a tail that is shorter than their body.

853.

Chinese hamsters have a distinctive stripe running along their back, from the neck to the base of the tail.

854.

They come in various color variations, including brown, gray, black, and white.

855.

Chinese hamsters are nocturnal animals, meaning they are most active during the night and sleep during the day.

856.

They have relatively long lifespans compared to other hamster species, typically living for 2-3 years.

857.

Chinese hamsters have a gentle and docile temperament, making them suitable pets for children and adults alike.

858.

They are solitary animals and should be housed individually to prevent territorial conflicts.

859.

Chinese hamsters are excellent climbers and can scale the sides of their enclosure using their sharp claws.

860.

They are known for their exceptional jumping ability, often leaping from one surface to another.

861.

Chinese hamsters are omnivorous, consuming a diet that consists of seeds, grains, fruits, vegetables, and occasionally small insects.

862.

They have specialized cheek pouches that allow them to carry and store food for later consumption.

863.

Chinese hamsters have a high metabolism and require a balanced and nutritious diet to maintain optimal health.

864.

They are skilled burrowers, creating intricate tunnels and chambers in bedding materials to create their nests.

865.

Chinese hamsters are known for their agility and dexterity, often displaying acrobatic behaviors while exploring their environment.

866.

They have a keen sense of smell and use their nose to locate food and detect potential predators.

867.

Chinese hamsters are relatively low-maintenance pets, requiring a clean and spacious cage, fresh food, and water.

868.

They are sensitive to extreme temperatures and should be kept in a controlled environment between 65-75°F (18-24°C).

869.

Chinese hamsters have a reproductive period of around 8-12 months, and females can have several litters throughout their lifetime.

870.

The gestation period for Chinese hamsters is approximately 18-21 days, after which the female gives birth to a litter of 3-12 pups.

871.

Chinese hamster pups are born blind and hairless but develop rapidly, opening their eyes within 14 days and becoming independent after 3-4 weeks.

872.

They have relatively short breeding cycles, with females capable of mating shortly after giving birth.

873.

Chinese hamsters have a natural instinct for hoarding food and will often stash extra food in various locations within their enclosure.

874.

They have a gentle and delicate nature, requiring careful handling to avoid injury.

875.

Chinese hamsters are clean animals and spend a significant amount of time grooming their fur to maintain its cleanliness and texture.

876.

They communicate through a variety of vocalizations, including squeaks, chirps, and soft clicking sounds.

877.

Chinese hamsters have a curious and exploratory nature, often investigating new objects and environments.

878.

They are adept at escaping their enclosures if not securely contained, so it's essential to provide a secure and escape-proof habitat.

879.

Chinese hamsters have incisors that continuously grow throughout their lives, necessitating access to chew toys and hard materials to wear down their teeth.

880.

They have a natural instinct for digging, so providing them with a suitable substrate, such as sand or shredded paper, allows them to engage in this behavior.

881.

Chinese hamsters are relatively quiet pets, making them suitable for individuals living in apartments or shared spaces.

882.

They have a relatively low odor compared to other small pets, but regular cleaning of their enclosure is still necessary to maintain a clean and odor-free environment.

883.

Chinese hamsters have delicate respiratory systems and can be sensitive to dust and strong odors, so it's important to provide a clean and well-ventilated habitat.

884.

They are naturally inquisitive and can be trained to perform simple tricks or navigate through obstacle courses.

885.

Chinese hamsters are susceptible to certain health issues, including dental problems, respiratory infections, and obesity, so regular veterinary check-ups are essential.

886.

They have a good sense of balance and can walk along narrow ledges and ropes with ease.

887.

Chinese hamsters have a relatively low water requirement, obtaining most of their hydration from fresh fruits and vegetables.

888.

They are agile climbers and can make use of vertical spaces within their enclosure, including ramps and branches.

889.

Chinese hamsters have a relatively short mating ritual, with the male performing a "mating dance" to attract the female.

890.

They are naturally curious about their surroundings and enjoy the stimulation of toys and enrichment activities.

891.

Chinese hamsters have a well-developed sense of hearing and can detect sounds at high frequencies.

892.

They have a strong sense of territory and may display territorial behaviors, such as scent marking and defending their living space.

893.

Chinese hamsters are known to be meticulous nest builders, creating cozy nests using materials such as shredded paper, hay, and bedding.

894.

They are agile jumpers and can leap impressive distances, both horizontally and vertically.

895.

Chinese hamsters have a remarkable ability to squeeze through small openings due to their flexible bodies.

896.

They have relatively small bladders, leading to frequent urination and the need for regular cage cleaning.

897.

Chinese hamsters are social animals and enjoy human interaction, although they may be shy or skittish at first.

898.

They have a keen sense of balance and can maintain stability while walking on uneven or narrow surfaces.

899.

Chinese hamsters have a rapid metabolism, requiring frequent feeding to meet their energy needs.

900.

They are fascinating creatures with unique behaviors and characteristics, making them a popular choice as pets for hamster enthusiasts.

901.

Commander's House is a historic structure located within the Fort Ross State Historic Park in California.

902.

It was built in 1812 by Russian fur traders and served as the residence for the fort's commanders.

903.

The house is a two-story wooden structure with a traditional Russian design, featuring a steeply pitched roof and wrap-around porches.

904.

Commander's House is one of the few remaining examples of Russian colonial architecture in the United States.

905.

It is constructed from locally sourced materials, including redwood and fir.

906.

The interior of the house showcases traditional Russian furnishings and decor, giving visitors a glimpse into the life of the fort's commanders.

907.

The house originally had eight rooms, including living quarters, a dining room, and offices.

908.

Commander's House served as the administrative center of Fort Ross and played a crucial role in the management of the Russian-American Company's fur trading operations.

909.

The house provided housing and accommodation for various Russian commanders who oversaw the fort's activities.

910.

Commander's House also served as a place for official meetings and gatherings with Native American tribes and other visiting dignitaries.

911.

It was the focal point of the fort's social life, hosting celebrations, dances, and cultural events.

912.

The house was built to withstand the harsh coastal climate, with its sturdy construction and reinforced walls.

913.

Commander's House is located in a picturesque setting overlooking the Pacific Ocean, offering stunning views of the surrounding landscape.

914.

The fort and Commander's House became part of the California State Park system in 1906.

915.

The house has undergone several restoration projects over the years to preserve its historic integrity.

916.

Today, Commander's House serves as a museum and interpretive center, showcasing exhibits and artifacts related to the Russian-American Company and the history of Fort Ross.

917.

Visitors can explore the various rooms of the house, including the commander's office, bedrooms, and the dining area.

918.

The house is furnished with period-appropriate furniture, artwork, and household items to recreate the atmosphere of the early 19th century.

919.

Interpretive displays provide insights into the daily life of the fort's inhabitants and the cultural exchange between the Russians and Native American tribes.

920.

The surrounding gardens and landscape feature native plant species and provide a serene and peaceful environment for visitors to enjoy.

921.

Commander's House is listed on the National Register of Historic Places, recognizing its significance in American history.

922.

It is considered a significant cultural and architectural landmark in California, representing the multicultural heritage of the region.

923.

The fort and Commander's House are part of a larger preservation effort to safeguard the historical legacy of Russian settlement in North America.

924.

The house stands as a testament to the early Russian presence in California and the complex interactions between European settlers and Native American communities.

925.

Over the years, Commander's House has been a focal point for historical research and academic study, contributing to our understanding of early Russian-American history.

926.

The house provides educational programs and guided tours for visitors, offering a deeper appreciation of the fort's history and cultural significance.

927.

Commander's House is a popular destination for tourists interested in California's rich history and the unique heritage of Russian colonization.

928.

The fort and Commander's House are situated within a stunning natural landscape, providing opportunities for hiking, picnicking, and enjoying the outdoors.

929.

The house has been featured in various films, documentaries, and television shows, attracting attention to its historical significance.

930.

Commander's House stands as a symbol of cross-cultural exchange and the resilience of early settlers in adapting to new environments.

931.

It serves as a reminder of the challenges and triumphs experienced by those who sought to establish a presence in the remote corners of the world.

932.

The restoration and preservation of Commander's House have been supported by community organizations, preservation societies, and government entities dedicated to safeguarding cultural heritage.

933.

The house offers a glimpse into the unique blend of Russian and Native American cultures that emerged from the interactions at Fort Ross.

934.

Commander's House is surrounded by the remnants of other structures from the fort's heyday, including the Russian Orthodox chapel and various outbuildings.

935.

The fort and its buildings, including Commander's House, have been recognized as a National Historic Landmark, signifying their exceptional historical significance.

936.

The house has witnessed a significant period of change in California's history, from its Russian ownership to subsequent Mexican and American control.

937.

Commander's House serves as a touchstone for ongoing cultural exchanges between Russia and the United States, fostering dialogue and understanding.

938.

The house represents an important chapter in the exploration and colonization of the Pacific Northwest, contributing to our understanding of early maritime history.

939.

Commander's House is a point of pride for the local community, representing their shared heritage and serving as a gathering place for cultural events and celebrations.

940.

The house has inspired artists, writers, and photographers who have captured its unique beauty and historical significance.

941.

Commander's House has been the subject of archaeological investigations and historical research, uncovering new insights into the lives of those who lived and worked at Fort Ross.

942.

The house has been resilient in the face of natural disasters and the passage of time, standing as a testament to the craftsmanship and durability of its construction.

943.

Commander's House offers visitors an immersive experience, allowing them to step back in time and imagine life at the fort during its active years.

944.

The house has a distinctive architectural style that blends Russian and California influences, reflecting the adaptive nature of settlers in new environments.

945.

Commander's House has been a site for cultural events and reenactments, providing a living history experience for visitors.

946.

The fort and Commander's House have been a source of inspiration for historical fiction and storytelling, capturing the imagination of writers and readers alike.

947.

The house has been a site of pilgrimage for descendants of Russian settlers and Native American tribes, who seek to reconnect with their ancestral roots.

948.

Commander's House has witnessed the ebb and flow of human history, serving as a silent witness to the passage of time and the changes that have shaped the region.

949.

The house has been a subject of preservation efforts, with ongoing maintenance and restoration projects ensuring its long-term survival for future generations to enjoy.

950.

Commander's House stands as a living legacy, reminding us of the interconnectedness of cultures and the enduring significance of shared histories.

951.

Coso Rock Art District is located in the eastern Sierra Nevada Mountains of California.

952.

It is recognized as one of the most significant rock art sites in North America.

953.

The rock art in the Coso Rock Art District dates back thousands of years, with some images believed to be over 10,000 years old.

954.

The district spans over 4,000 acres and contains more than 100,000 rock art images.

955.

The rock art at Coso includes petroglyphs (carvings) and pictographs (paintings) made by indigenous peoples.

956.

The images depict a wide range of subjects, including animals, human figures, celestial symbols, geometric patterns, and abstract designs.

957.

The rock art provides insights into the cultural practices, spiritual beliefs, and daily life of the indigenous peoples who inhabited the area.

958.

The Coso Rock Art District has been a site of archaeological research since the early 20th century.

959.

The rock art is created on basalt boulders and cliffs using stone tools, chisels, and pigments made from natural materials.

960.

The site was added to the National Register of Historic Places in 1973, recognizing its cultural and historical significance.

961.

The rock art is spread across several different locations within the district, including the China Lake Naval Air Weapons Station.

962.

The rock art is incredibly detailed and intricate, showcasing the skill and artistic ability of the ancient inhabitants.

963.

The Coso Rock Art District is managed by the Bureau of Land Management (BLM) to protect and preserve the site.

964.

The rock art is culturally significant to the Native American tribes in the region, who continue to have a spiritual connection to the site.

965.

The rock art provides a window into the past, allowing us to study and understand the cultural heritage of the indigenous peoples.

966.

The Coso Rock Art District is open to the public, and visitors can explore designated areas to view the rock art.

967.

Interpretive signs and guides provide information about the rock art and its historical context.

968.

The rock art is susceptible to damage from weathering, vandalism, and human interaction, so conservation efforts are essential.

969.

The district is home to one of the largest concentrations of petroglyphs in the Western Hemisphere.

970.

The Coso Rock Art District is a UNESCO World Heritage Site candidate, highlighting its global significance.

971.

The rock art images are believed to have multiple meanings, ranging from religious and ceremonial to historical and artistic expressions.

972.

The rock art includes depictions of animals such as bighorn sheep, deer, rabbits, birds, and snakes, reflecting the diverse wildlife of the region.

973.

The rock art also portrays human figures engaged in various activities, such as hunting, dancing, and gathering.

974.

Some of the rock art images may have astronomical and calendrical significance, aligning with celestial events.

975.

The Coso Rock Art District is an important site for archaeological study, helping researchers understand the migration patterns and cultural interactions of ancient peoples.

976.

The rock art serves as a cultural heritage site for Native American tribes, who maintain a connection to their ancestral traditions and stories.

977.

The Coso Rock Art District is a sacred place for many Native American tribes, and certain areas may have restricted access or require permission for visitation.

978.

The rock art provides a visual record of the changing environment and climatic conditions over thousands of years.

979.

The site offers a glimpse into the spiritual beliefs and mythologies of the indigenous peoples, as some images depict deities or supernatural beings.

980.

The Coso Rock Art District has inspired artists, scholars, and researchers from various disciplines to study and interpret the significance of the rock art.

981.

The rock art is considered an important cultural resource and has been the subject of ongoing documentation and documentation efforts.

982.

The district serves as an outdoor museum, showcasing the richness and diversity of Native American cultural heritage.

983.

The rock art images may have been created for ceremonial or educational purposes, serving as teaching tools for passing down cultural knowledge.

984.

The Coso Rock Art District is part of a larger cultural landscape that includes other archaeological sites, cultural features, and natural resources.

985.

The rock art is found in different styles, reflecting the artistic traditions and influences of different periods in history.

986.

The district offers opportunities for research and collaboration between archaeologists, anthropologists, historians, and indigenous communities.

987.

The rock art provides a connection to the past for contemporary indigenous communities, reinforcing their cultural identity and resilience.

988.

The site has been used for educational purposes, allowing students and researchers to study the rock art and learn about Native American history and culture.

989.

The Coso Rock Art District has been featured in documentaries, publications, and exhibitions, raising awareness about its importance.

990.

The rock art serves as a reminder of the enduring legacy of indigenous peoples and their contributions to the cultural heritage of the region.

991.

The district's conservation efforts include monitoring, erosion control measures, and educational programs to promote responsible visitation.

992.

The rock art images have different styles and motifs that reflect the artistic preferences and cultural diversity of the ancient inhabitants.

993.

Some rock art images may contain symbols and iconography that have deep spiritual and cultural meanings.

994.

The Coso Rock Art District attracts visitors from around the world who are interested in ancient civilizations and the preservation of cultural heritage.

995.

The rock art images provide clues about the social structure, economic activities, and technological advancements of the indigenous peoples.

996.

The site has been a subject of ongoing research and debate, with experts exploring different interpretations and theories about the rock art's meaning.

997.

The rock art is a testament to the enduring artistic expression of the indigenous peoples, as the images have survived for thousands of years.

998.

The Coso Rock Art District has been an important site for cultural revitalization efforts, as indigenous communities work to preserve their traditions and reconnect with their ancestral roots.

999.

The rock art serves as a reminder of the interconnectedness between humans and the natural world, highlighting the deep relationship that indigenous peoples had with their environment.

1000.

The Coso Rock Art District is a cultural treasure that provides a window into the past, fostering appreciation and respect for the rich indigenous heritage of the region.

www.ingramcontent.com/pod-product-compliance
Lightning Source LLC
Chambersburg PA
CBHW072246260726
48659CB00004BA/1432